P9-ASK-574

Janet Shannon

Human Aging and Dying
A STUDY IN SOCIOCULTURAL GERONTOLOGY

CARNEGIE LIBRARY
LIVINGSTONE COLLEGE
SALISBURY, NC 28144

Human Aging and Dying

A STUDY IN SOCIOCULTURAL GERONTOLOGY

WILBUR H. WATSON
ROBERT J. MAXWELL
EDITORS

ST. MARTIN'S PRESS
New York

Library of Congress Catalog Card Number: 76-28130
Copyright © 1977 by St. Martin's Press, Inc.
All Rights Reserved.
Manufactured in the United States of America.
0987
fedcba
For information, write: St. Martin's Press, Inc.,
175 Fifth Avenue, New York, N.Y. 10010

cover design: Mies Hora

cloth ISBN: 312-39690-2
paper ISBN: 312-39725-9

Acknowledgments

CHAPTER 2 "Information and Esteem: Cultural Considerations in the Treatment of the Aged" is based on a revision of an article by Robert J. Maxwell and Philip Silverman which previously appeared under the same title in *Aging and Human Development*, vol. 1, no. 4, October 1970, pages 361–392. Used with the permission of the publisher, Dorchester, Mass.

CHAPTER 3 "The Changing Status of Elders in a Polynesian Society" is based on a revision of an article by Robert J. Maxwell which previously appeared under the same title in *Aging and Human Development*, vol. 1, no. 2, April 1970, pages 137–146. Used with the permission of the publisher, Dorchester, Mass.

CHAPTER 4 "Aging and Race" is a greatly revised version of an article by Wilbur H. Watson which previously appeared under the same title in *Social Action*, vol. 38, no. 3, November 1971, pages 20–30. Used with the permission of Council for Christian Social Action, United Church of Christ as publisher.

CHAPTER 5 was based on:
"Territory and Self in a Geriatric Setting" by Robert J. Maxwell, Jeanne E. Bader, and Wilbur H. Watson which appeared in *The Gerontologist*, vol. 12, no. 4, Winter 1972, pages 413–417.
"Institutional Structures of Aging and Dying" by Wilbur H. Watson, in *Environmental Research and Aging*. Washington, D.C.: The Gerontological Society, 1974, pages 39–66. Used with the permission of the publisher.

PREFACE

A medical interest in the aged has existed for many years, because the elderly, more than any other group, are plagued by both infectious and degenerative disease. However, scientific interest in the social and psychological behavior of the aged is more recent. For example, the Gerontological Society, the major professional organization in the United States dealing with the subject of aging, was organized as recently as 1948. Since its inception, although not necessarily because of it, there have been four major areas of study: (1) medical and psychiatric aspects of aging, (2) measurement of changes in attitudinal patterns and psychological characteristics in association with aging, (3) studies of changes in life styles, family and community behavior, and social status in relation to aging, and (4) studies of mutual adaptations of agents of health and welfare institutions and the impaired elderly in family and community settings.

In the rapidly growing body of gerontological literature, sociological studies have largely focused on (1) demographic and intergenerational distributions of elderly persons and (2) studies of aging in relation to retirement and social organization in various societies. Few encounter-oriented ethnographies exist which present first-hand accounts of daily living and coping behavior in old age. Furthermore, anthropology, in its restricted definition as the study of non-Western societies, has almost ignored aging in either the particular or cross-cultural sense.

It is difficult to understand why social scientists have been so late in turning research attention to the problems of aging and the aged, but it is easy to understand why this unfortunate state of affairs is now being altered. The factors that now compel the study of the elderly by modern social scientists include (1) mounting numbers of aged-related health and welfare policy questions along with an increased recognition of the scarcity of carefully documented information, (2) more support for aged-related research in governmental funding patterns, and (3) growing demand for low-cost, high-quality special services associated with the increasing numbers and longevity of people in old age.

Human Aging and Dying has three aims: (1) to help fill the void created by the lack of ethnographic data on the organization of behavior in old age, (2) to describe various methods and problems associated with field studies of aging and social behavior, and (3) to develop implications for theory and social policy and directions for further study in social gerontology.

W. H. W.
R. J. M.

ACKNOWLEDGMENTS

A number of people have provided invaluable assistance in the realization of the research reported in this book. Although it is impossible to name everyone who played a part, there are some persons who must be singled out.

Among the most important is Philip Silverman who helped considerably in carrying out the study described in chapter 2. His participation in the development of the theoretical framework was essential, and he was primarily responsible for the design and the actual implementation of the study. Under Professor Silverman's guidance, the students in his cross-cultural methodology course, given at the City College of New York, CUNY, Spring, 1970, did most of the coding. Particularly important were the contributions of Dorothy Burstyn and Mary McMecham. Pertti J. Pelto, John M. Roberts, and Frank W. Young were also helpful in the preparation of that chapter.

Chapter 3 depended on so many informants that a list would include virtually all of the residents of Vaitogi Village, Tutuila. However, Auau Foe, Chief of Tualauta County, American Samoa, must be mentioned for his support throughout the research.

Melvin Turner, National Caucus on the Black Aged, Inc., and Daniel Stone, Administration on Aging, HEW, are acknowledged for stimulating discussions and providing access to data that helped to motivate a study of "ethnic correlates of longevity and aging behavior" (1970-1971) on which chapter 4 is based. Hobart Jackson, Hyacinth Graham, Junius Rhone, Izzora Scott, and Brenda Anderson of The Stephen Smith Geriatric Center were also helpful at various stages of the research from which chapters 4, 5, and 6 were developed. Without their support, the research necessary for the writing of chapter 6 would not have been possible.

Most of the research reported in part II was supported by grants, research assistants, seminars, and research settings made possible through the Departments of Sociology, Anthropology, and The Center for Urban Ethnography of the University of Pennsylvania and the Philadelphia Geriatric Center (1968-1972). Erving Goffman, Renee C. Fox, Otto Pollak,

John Szwed, and Philip Rieff of the University of Pennsylvania provided major intellectual and research incentive during the early phases of the studies from which we developed the chapters on "The Disabled, The Dying, and Their Keepers." We are grateful to the Center for Urban Ethnography and The National Institute of Mental Health, for PHS Grant #MH 17216, 1970–1972.

M. Powell Lawton, Arthur Waldman, and Bernard Leibowitz of the Philadelphia Geriatric Center provided permission for use of the research facilities of that institution as well as partial support through grant #HS 00100, Health Services and Mental Health Administration. We are thankful for the many hours of stimulating discussions with members of the research staff at the center, among whom Jeanne Bader must be singled out for her assistance in the collection and preliminary analysis of some of the data presented in chapter 5.

Without the manuscript typing and stylistic editing of Suzanne Vargus, Sheri Deseretz, Eileen Trombetta, and Grace Dessureau, and the tolerance of our families for our frequently irregular working hours, this book could not have been brought to fruition at this time. Finally, we are grateful to our editors at St. Martin's Press for their encouragement and care in preparing our manuscript for publication.

CONTENTS

Human Aging and Dying
A STUDY IN SOCIOCULTURAL GERONTOLOGY

INTRODUCTION | 1

The number of people 65 years of age and older in the United States increased from 4.1 percent in 1900 to about 9.5 percent in 1970 (Riley et al. 1971: 16-24). During the same period, the absolute number of old people in the United States increased from 3.1 million to about 19.6 million.

Since 1900 there has been an enormous increase in the number of old people in other countries as well. Of course, a different age structure prevails in less industrialized countries, ordinarily characterized by a higher birth rate and many children, few of whom survive to old age (Cahn 1969). It is likely that as these countries complete what has come to be called "the demographic transition"—the switch from high birth and high death rates to low birth and low death rates—their age structures will become similar to that of the United States.

As the elderly population increases so does the incidence of their everyday difficulties increase. For example, in the United States growing numbers of old people suffer from chronic brain syndrome (Lowenthal 1964). These people constitute a subpopulation of the elderly with known and irreversible brain damage characterized by cognitive, behavioral, and social impairments (Kleban et al 1971; Brody et al 1971). Although the majority of older people function relatively well outside of specialized institutional settings (Shanas 1969), and only about 5 percent of the total population over 65 is institutionalized (see the 1970 census), it is quite clear that a growing

1

number of old people have severe physical and mental impairment requiring long-term care. If at any given time only about 5 percent of the over-65 population is institutionalized, an even higher proportion of those outside specialized residential settings spend at least *some* part of their lives in institutions, such as hospitals, with acute or chronic illness. Since custodial care in the home has been associated traditionally with a rural rather than an urban life-style, and since nuclear families are replacing extended families, there is little reason to anticipate any decline in the percentage of the institutionalized aged. In fact, we should expect quite the opposite. Care of the aged is simply one of many functions which are no longer the responsibility of the nuclear family.

Among the problems that further confront the elderly in this country are inordinately low incomes, poor housing, and a lack of safe, easily used public transportation. There is also a stigma attached to aging, along with a risk of social rejection and personal degradation.

Social Reactions to the Elderly

There is a point at which human beings, if they live long enough, probably will be defined socially, and personally, as "old." Although this situation is widespread, little value or attractiveness is attached to age as a goal. Why does old age become a time of tranquility for some but a time of despair for others? The declining physical and psychological powers in old age cannot be the entire answer because such changes occur in the aging of all individuals. The perceptions of old people and their subsequent treatment by others, however, vary from place to place and from time to time. Such variations would seem to have a great deal to do with the value placed on elderly persons (McTavish 1971).

Social devaluations of people in old age may be related to changes in physical appearances and abilities which are considered negative deviations from the society's ideals. As suggested by Goffman (1963) the bodily signs of elderly individuals, like those of the blind, the black, and the severely mentally disabled, may become subject to stigmatization signifying, as it were, that there is something unusual and "wrong" about the individual.

The evidences of disease, physical disability, and old age, however, are not stigmas in all societies. For example, among the Kubu of Sumatra, minor diseases, skin eruptions, wounds, or similar ailments did not in themselves result in negative social reactions (Sigerist 1943: 67). There, the criteria for determining disability were social, not physical. As long as individuals were able to perform in accordance with tribal rules, their physical condition was not considered a critical factor in determining their ability to function in the group. If, however, a person became host to a disease such as smallpox, and was no longer able to perform expected functions in the group, noticeable negative reactions would be drawn from others, including kin. Once he was considered unable to carry on expected social performances, the following occurred:

> All [would]·avoid him as they would a corpse, making his isolation complete. The sufferer is dead, socially, long before physical death has overtaken him (Sigerist 1943: 67).

Similar. to the Kubu, social behavior in ancient Greece clearly indicated the social position of able and disabled members.

> The Greek world was a world of the healthy and sound. To the Greek of the 5th century B.C., and long thereafter, health appeared as the highest good. Disease was a great curse. Disease, by removing a person from his place of perfection, made of him an inferior being. The sick, the cripple and the weakling could expect consideration from society only so long as their condition was capable of improvement (Sigerist 1943: 133).

Relative to failings in physical and in moral character, social reactions to those considered mad during the European Age of Reason (1656–1800) were largely influenced by concerns about how the visibility of a mad person would blemish or befoul the public image of the family or relatives (Foucault 1965: 62). When social befoulment was anticipated, or when a family's honor was threatened by a member whose appearance or behavior was without social virtue, confinement was indicated. Under these circumstances, confinement could continue until the individual's social disability was no longer manifest or until it no longer constituted a threat to the prestige of family members.

> Confinement is a right of families seeking to escape dishonor. "That which is called a base action is placed in the rank of those which public order does not permit us to tolerate. . . . It seems that the honor of a family requires the disappearance from society of the individual who by vile and abject habits shames his relatives." Inversely, liberation is in order when

the danger of scandal is past and the honor of families or of the Church can no longer be sullied (Foucault 1965: 64).

Unlike the Renaissance, when individuals were permitted considerable rein to act out forms of so-called unreason in the light of day, public display of bizarre behavior was not permissible during the Age of Reason.[1] The inference may be drawn from prohibitions against public display of unreasonable behavior that it was disconcerting to others.

Confinement, or segregation, persists even today as a way for "self-proclaimed normals" to cope with their own uneasiness by shielding themselves against the demands of caring for the severely impaired elderly (Townsend 1964: 159–163; Lowenthal 1964: 22–36). Historically, rationalizations for segregation of the stigmatized have ranged from (1) admonitions as to what would result from undue mixing of the sacred and the profane; (2) beliefs that the stigmatized are fixed in a state of inverse exaltation, their disability and confinement sanctioned by God's will; and (3) beliefs that it is imperative to protect a family's honor, even if that means removing from its presence and from public scrutiny a socially disabled member; to (4) the need to protect the stigmatized from harming themselves or being harmed by others. While these issues emerge periodically in all the sociocultural considerations in this study of aging and social behavior, we also discuss the social organization of settings specialized for the care of the elderly in modern American society.

The foregoing historical sketch of social reactions to aging and socially disabled persons is admittedly brief. It does not cover the range of social reactions to aging and/or social disability that could be described in a detailed study of the history of aging and health care in several societies. Nor was that our aim. This brief statement was intended as a modest introduction to some of the specific issues raised in our studies and to our approach to sociocultural gerontology. An overview of our analytic framework will help to show the conceptual linkages between the various studies that follow.

The Analytic Framework in Sociocultural Gerontology

Aging and dying can be construed in several complementary ways: (1) coextensive events in the unfolding of a biological template, (2) a sequence of developmental psychosocial events, and (3) behaviors related to developmental status passages in a larger sociocultural system from which their meanings are ultimately derived. This third perspective constitutes our general frame of reference. Our chief concern throughout is contextual analysis.

The experiences we undergo as we age and die are not simply biological events, but they are in several ways defined and regulated for us by members of our society. Long before our own senescence, we develop a reasonably good idea about the drama of life that is enacted in old age (Kastenbaum 1969; Kalish 1969). As adolescents, young adults, and middle agers, we contribute to the systems of thought and social behavior that unfold during our lifetimes, and these systems help to determine the significances of old age by which our own senescence will be judged. Through our own lives and through the study of others we acquire some notion of the circumstances in which we are likely to die.

For an increasing number of people in the United States, dying will occur in a sterile and unfamiliar hospital, among unfamiliar odors and strangers dressed in uniform white and O.R. green (Brody 1973). In old age, many people express uncertainty and fright when contemplating their personal and social identity and their ability to go on living independently. Their uneasiness is not simply because death is imminent, although that is always significant. Of equal significance is (1) their uncertainty about the nature of their dying (Kubler–Ross 1970), (2) the social and psychological supports that can be expected from family and friends in the course of their dying, and (3) the behavior that family and friends will expect of the elderly in their final days.

American Indians of the eastern woodlands knew how they were to die. They were to sing their individual death songs as long as they could. If they were being tortured to death by their enemies, during pauses in their death songs they were to taunt the captors for lacking imagination (e.g., Brandon 1961: 170).

Among Tibetans, the role of the dying was highly structured. As described in their Book of the Dead (1907), an instructor was to sit and whisper into the ear of the dying person a series of verses or Bardoes, describing what was to be experienced during the several stages of dying—ending, it was believed, in a union with the Almighty.

Social definitions cover not only the role of the dying person but the character of the dead. Depending on the system of beliefs, after death one may become a ghost, be reincarnated, enter a supernatural kingdom, or enter any of a variety of other forms, any of which can be understood as acquiring its significance and structure from the society in which the beliefs are institutionalized. Whatever else death-related beliefs stand for, they certainly signify something about human hopes and preoccupations with the prospects for an existence without end. Functionally, these beliefs may lessen the anxieties attendant upon dying.

Inescapable biological and experiential considerations are also involved with aging and dying. However, there is no point in raising again the sterile argument that one or another set of determinants at one or another level of analysis is primary in the study of human behavior. After all, culture, society, personality, and organism are jointly influential in determining human behavior. Each level of analysis may be treated separately or in relation to one or more of the other systems in the study of behavior.

Summary

The approach here focuses on society and culture as the starting points for analyzing human aging and dying. We treat society (the people and their relationships) and culture (the body of custom) as inseparable features of organized human groups. We define the sociocultural system as the customs and relations that bind people together in networks of relationships. Our focus on sociocultural systems is based on our observation that not enough attention has been directed toward aging and dying as sociocultural events. Since biological aspects of old age are relatively constant in effect, although varying with longevity and instances of morbidity from one individual to the next, we examine the correspondences between sociocultural context, social definitions and reactions to aging and dying, and social psychological behavior of old people. Our interpretive framework, then, adopts the sociocultural system as the initial level of analysis and examines the influence of differing contexts upon the processes of aging and dying.

Part one treats some of the factors that contribute to enhancing or weakening an old person's status in sociocultural systems. Being socially defined as healthy rather than infirm, or vigorous rather than enfeebled, can decisively affect the treatment that kinsmen and neighbors extend.

Part two deals with small groups of the elderly in two specific settings who have been socially and/or personally defined as unable to maintain themselves in an open sociocultural system and have been assigned residential space in specialized institutions. The concept of open sociocultural systems is detailed in chapter 2. From a sociocultural perspective, any notion of social disability is specific to a context and is rooted in the changing demands made upon older persons in relation to other members of a group.

The last chapter deals with dying, the final performance for us all. Perhaps paradoxically, dying is a situation in which the elderly, more than any other age group, are likely to organize a successful response.

Notes

1. During the Renaissance it was believed that "public outrage gave evil the powers of example and redemption." See M. Foucault, *Madness and Civilization* (New York: New American Library, 1965).

References

Becker, Howard S., and Anselm L. Strauss. "Careers, Personality, and Adult Socialization." *American Journal of Sociology*, 62, 3 (November 1956).

Brandon, William. *The American Book of Indians*. New York: Dell, 1961.

Brody, Elaine M., Morton H. Kleban, M. Powell Lawton, and Herbert Silverman. "Excess Disabilities of Mentally Impaired Aged: Impact of Individualized Treatment." *The Gerontologist*, Part 1 (Summer 1971), 124–133.

Brody, Stanley J. A Trialogue with Mary Hanlan and Doris A. Howell on Serious Illness and Dying. (The Ars Moriendi Conference on Resources for Death, Dying and Serious Illness.) Norristown State Hospital, Norristown, Pa., November 16, 1973.

Burgess, Ernest W., ed. *Aging in Western Societies*. Chicago: University of Chicago Press, 1960.

Cahn, Edgar S., ed. *Our Brother's Keeper: The Indian in White America*. New York: New Community Press, 1969.

Clark, Margaret. "The Anthropology of Aging: A New Area for Studies of Culture and Personality." *The Gerontologist*, 7, 1 (March 1967).

Foucault, Michel. *Madness and Civilization: A History of Insanity in the Age of Reason*. New York: New American Library, 1965.

Goffman, E. *Stigma: Notes on the Management of Spoiled Identity.* Englewood Cliffs, N.J.: Prentice-Hall, 1963.

Havighurst, R. J., J. M. A. Munnichs, B. L. Neugarten, and H. Thomas, eds. *Adjustment to Retirement: A Cross-National Study.* Assen, Netherlands: Koninklijke van Gorcum, 1969.

Jackson, J. J. "Social Gerontology and the Negro: A Review." *The Gerontologist,* 7, 3, Part 1 (September 1967), 168–178.

―――. "Kinship Relations Among Older Negro Americans." Paper presented at the 8th International Congress of Gerontology, Washington, D.C., August 25, 1969.

Kalish, Richard A. "The Effects of Death upon the Family." In Leonard Pearson, ed., *Death and Dying.* Cleveland: Press of Case Western Reserve University, 1969.

Kastenbaum, Robert. "Psychological Death." In Leonard Pearson, ed., *Death and Dying.* Cleveland: Press of Case Western Reserve University, 1969.

Kleban, Morton H., Elaine M. Brody, and M. Powell Lawton. "Personality Traits in the Mentally-Impaired Aged and Their Relationship to Improvements in Current Functioning." *The Gerontologist,* 11, 2, Part 1 (Summer 1971), 133–140.

―――, and ―――. "Prediction of Improvement in Mentally Impaired Aged: Personality Ratings by Social Workers." *Journal of Gerontology,* 27, 1 (1972), 69–76.

Kubler-Ross, Elisabeth. *On Death and Dying.* New York: Macmillan, 1970.

Lawton, M. Powell, and Morton H. Kleban. "The Aged Resident of the Inner City." *The Gerontologist,* 11, 4, Part 1 (Winter 1971), 277–283.

Lindsay, Inabel B. "The Multiple Hazards of Age and Race: The Situation of Aged Blacks in the United States" (A Working Paper prepared for the Special Committee on Aging, U.S. Senate). Washington, D.C.: Government Printing Office, 1971.

Lowenthal, Marjorie Fisk. *Lives in Distress.* New York: Basic Books, 1964.

―――, Paul L. Berkman, and Associates. *Aging and Mental Disorder in San Francisco: A Social Psychiatric Study.* San Francisco: Jossey-Bass, 1967.

McTavish, D. G. "Perceptions of Old People: A Review of Research Methodologies and Findings." *The Gerontologist,* 2, 4, Part 2 (1971), 90–102.

Neugarten, Bernice L., ed. *Middle Age and Aging.* Chicago: University of Chicago Press, 1968.

Poe, William D. *The Old Person in Your Home.* New York: Scribner's, 1969.

Riley, M. W., A. Foner, B. Hess, and M. L. Toby. "Socialization for the Middle and Later Years." In D. A. Goslin, ed. *Handbook of Socialization Theory and Research.* Chicago: Rand McNally, 1969.

―――, M. E. Johnson, and A. Foner. *A Sociology of Age Stratification.* New York: Russell Sage Foundation, 1971.

Rosow, Irwin. *Social Integration of the Aged.* New York: Free Press, 1967.

Shanas, Ethel. *Old People in Three Industrial Societies.* New York: Atherton Press, 1968.

——. "Living Arrangements and Housing of Old People." In E. W. Busse and E. Pfeiffer, eds. *Behavior and Adaptation in Late Life.* Boston: Little, Brown, 1969.

Sigerist, Henry. *Civilization and Disease.* Chicago: University of Chicago Press, 1943.

Streib, Gordon F. "Intergenerational Relations: Perspectives of the Two Generations on the Older Parent." *Journal of Marriage and the Family,* 27 (1965), 469–476.

Tibbitts, Clark, ed. *Handbook of Social Gerontology.* Chicago: University of Chicago Press, 1960.

Townsend, Peter. *The Last Refuge.* London: Routledge and Kegan Paul, 1964.

——. *The Family Life of Old People.* New York: Free Press, 1957.

Worcester, Alfred. *The Care of the Aged the Dying and the Dead.* Springfield, Ill.: Thomas, 1961.

Part One

Aging as Status Passage in Comparative Social and Cross-Cultural Contexts

A status is a position in a group that can in theory be ascribed to or achieved by any given member and that carries for that member certain rewards and obligations. Entry into a socially approved status may give a group member a certain degree of prestige. This means that any given status is always defined and assigned importance in relation to other positions and to the system of values current in the group. For example, an organization of police officers is commonly charged with responsibility for enforcing a relatively specific body of ordinances or legal statutes.

In an organization of law enforcement officers, positions of authority are assigned to persons who must thereafter take responsibility for planning the recruitment, training, allocation of tasks, and supervision of work carried out by other members in the organization. New recruits are commonly assigned positions in the status hierarchy lower than the positions of officers who have been on the force for a longer time. Thus each position in a status hierarchy has a degree of prestige along with a corresponding degree of honor, deference, or authority for the person who occupies the position. However, honorific rights are not always straightforward in relation to a position in a social order.

Determinants of status honor vary widely within and between societies. In the United States, society is organized by traditional values and rules that approve male dominance in breadwinning for families and decision making in family-community relations. In such a society, females are likely to be assigned or trained to fill occupational and family positions that are less prestigious and less rewarded than the positions reserved for males. Similarly, black people in American politics, economics, and other forms of competitive enterprise are likely to receive less reward for their efforts than white people do. Both females and blacks occupy comparatively low status and are accorded significantly less status honor.

Age differences, like sex and race differences, can also influence status. For example, being middle aged or older in a society that exalts youth can induce the assignment of a low status. By contrast, in a society whose members exalt wisdom and believe that wisdom comes with age and experience, growing old can mean increasing status and prestige.

Not only do determinants of status vary according to the society, but status honor may vary with variations in rank on a particular dimension, such as age. As we shall see in the case studies of social reactions to persons entering old age, aging is associated with decreasing status honor in some societies and increasing honor in others.

Growing Old as Status Passage

When people join a group for the first time, or experience new age-related status positions, such as those that occur during transitions from childhood to adolescence or middle age to old age, they are assigned a status relative to others and to the social structure of the group. It is the process of personal mobility between and within groups, as well as the associated change in assigned rank, that we refer to by the term *status passage* (Glaser and Strauss 1968: 244). This is not mere change in position, nor is it mere movement from a position in one group to a corresponding position in another. The critical factor is change in the degree of prestige and honorific accord that becomes associated with change in position.

Any person may be perceived as elderly when compared to other members of his ethnic group who have not lived as long. An ethnic group is a collectivity of persons whose cultural background is similar, with traditions that include a relatively definite system of values, rules for everyday life, language or language group, and racial identity. While any comparison between groups based solely on chronological criteria may permit an unambiguous identification of their elderly members, longevity and social definitions of old age may vary among ethnic groups and influence the value and honor associated with age. Economic and age-related systems of values are the critical structural factors which guide judgments made about persons, such as the elderly, whose inability to maintain themselves may progress with time.

It is not mere chronological aging that is at issue here. It is *social aging*, defined by socially structured passages of persons into statuses that are related to chronology and performance. Once people enter old age, like any other status, the gatekeepers of the systems of values and rules in their society judge their abilities to live up to the roles associated with the position. The universality of age-related and ability-related determinants of social status accent the importance of the sociocultural approach to aging and dying as status passage processes.

By the criterion of the Administration on Aging of the U.S. Department of Health, Education and Welfare, Americans enter old age after living 60 years. However, many people here and throughout the world do not live to be 60 years of age. We can see this clearly if we look at data on average longevity among ethnic groups. For example, it was reported by Cahn (1969) that Alaskan Eskimos had an average life span of 39 years, and the longevity of American Indians on U.S. reservations averaged 44 years in 1968. Other data show that, on the average, blacks live to be 64.6 years of age (Davis 1971: 47) whereas whites live to 71 years of age. In each group women average somewhat longer lifespans than men.

There is no doubt that ethnic-related variations in expected longevity influence social definitions of old age. An elderly Sioux Indian may be chronologically younger than an elderly white Anglo-Saxon Protestant American but is ethnically old nevertheless. Longevity is the chronological yardstick against which ethnically specific variations and definitions of old age are measured. Against the background of the limits of longevity, known or intuited by members of any particular group, there are cultural and social variations in the reactions expressed and meanings assigned to persons defined as elderly or perceived as becoming elderly. It is to an analysis and discussion of comparative social and cross-cultural variations in these reactions to old age that we turn in the next three chapters.

References

Cahn, Edgar S., ed. *Our Brother's Keeper: The Indian in White America.* New York: New Community Press, 1969.

Davis, Donald L. "Growing Old Black." In *Employment Prospects of Aged Blacks, Chicanos, and Indians.* Washington, D.C.: National Council on the Aging, 1971.

Glaser, Barney G., and Anselm L. Strauss. *Time for Dying.* Chicago: Aldine, 1968.

INFORMATION AND ESTEEM: CULTURAL CONSIDERATIONS IN THE TREATMENT OF THE AGED | 2

Anthropologists have on the whole shown little interest in aging. With few exceptions, ethnographic reports mention the aged in passing, if at all, and then only in quite general statements. Thus the impression is conveyed that the population being studied is made up of mature men, with women and children as peripheral figures. Even culture and personality theorists, whose interest is in the various stages of the life cycle, give little attention to the aged. This neglect is odd, in view of the fact that, as Bromley (1966: 13) has pointed out, "we spend about one quarter of our lives growing up and three quarters growing old."

There are several reasons for this. Old age itself is not pleasant to contemplate. We would rather not be reminded of the biological changes associated with aging that someday we ourselves will undergo. Moreover, the aged occupy the terminal stage of the life cycle, so that we know where they will be twenty years from now, whereas we don't know exactly what will happen to the children in

NOTE: Philip Silverman, California State College, Bakersfield, was the co-author of this paper when it originally appeared as an article in *Aging and Human Development*, 1, 4 (1970), 361–393. His name appears here, rather than at the top of this page, solely in an attempt to enhance continuity. Professor Silverman is now principal investigator of a research project dealing with the activities and treatment of old people in a sample of 102 societies, which is both a more extensive and a much more intensive treatment of the general problem discussed in this chapter. His permission to reprint this slightly revised version of the earlier article is greatly appreciated.

the community. In this connection, old people are usually the guardians of tradition and not active agents of sociocultural change, so they are of lesser theoretical interest. Finally, there are few old people around in societies that are not relatively complex and industrialized.

Nevertheless, some descriptive material is available. Arensberg and Kimball (1940), Elwin's work on the Muria Gond (1947), Spencer on Samburu gerontocracy (1965), Clark and Anderson (1967) on aged representatives of various ethnic groups in the San Francisco Bay Area, and some more abbreviated efforts (see Cowgill 1965; Okada 1962a, 1962b; Rowe 1961; Shelton 1969) help to shed some light on the disposition of certain societies toward their older members.

Simmons's *The Role of the Aged in Primitive Society* (1945) deserves special mention as a more ambitious comparative work than the others. This volume stands as the first and only large-scale cross-cultural study of aging.[1] Rich as it is in illustrative material, it is unfortunately of limited value, largely because of its flawed methodology. In a sample of 71 societies, Simmons includes several that are closely related—for example, the Polar Eskimo and the Labrador Eskimo; the Dieri and the Aranda of Australia. With closely related societies, unlike closely related individuals, you don't know whether you are dealing with one case or two. In the absence of careful sampling procedures, generalizations drawn from the data may be awry. This alone would be enough to make Simmons's conclusions suspect, but, in addition, he coded 240 culture traits in these 71 societies without providing explicit coding rules so that the reliability of his data cannot be known. For example, he writes of "phallicism" without ever making his meaning plain. Finally, there are some errors in the statistical operations employed in the Simmons study which cast doubt on his other procedures (see, for example, his correlation 1, Appendix A, page 245).

In the years since the appearance of Simmons's book, the theory and methodology of comparative studies have come far, and it is perhaps time to reexamine the problem of the aged in cross-cultural perspective. A beginning was signaled by the appearance of Cowgill and Holmes's *Aging and Modernization* (1972).

It is suggested here that information of varying utility is distributed throughout any sociocultural system. In industrialized societies characterized by rapid sociocultural change, as well as by the storage of information in books, archives, computers, or other artifacts the information controlled by old people is rendered useless to society or—to the extent that it is useful—it is available elsewhere. Both rapid social change and information storage decrease the participation of the aged in the community's social life and so they become less important in terms of system maintenance and survival. This in turn causes respect for the aged to decline.

Sometimes in technologically simple societies the aged are killed or abandoned. This does not necessarily involve a loss of respect for the aged but it depends on severe ecological conditions—harsh environmental circumstances—where the group must conserve food or water. Under such conditions group survival may necessitate the sacrifice or abandonment of the aged in an effort to allow the young and strong to survive and reproduce.

It is hypothesized that societies can be arrayed along a continuum whose basis is the amount of useful information controlled by the aged. Accordingly, this informational control should be reflected in the participation of the aged in community affairs, and their participation should in turn determine the degree of esteem in which they are held by the other members of the community. This informational control and consequent social participation should decline with industrialization and its attendant rapid sociocultural change.

Theory

One of the more fruitful models developed for the investigation of human societies has focused on information storage and exchange and may be described under the general rubric of systems theory.

CULTURE AS A SYSTEM

If a system is a bounded organization of dynamically related components, then by definition any culture qualifies as a system. A sociocultural system is composed of units—individuals—who are organized into subsystems such as families, occupations, and other institutions. If the individuals in fact participate in the same sociocultural system (SCS), they are dynamically related, since the events that affect some of them will affect some or all of the others. To use terms developed in systems theory, interactions between members of the same SCS are governed by constraint. When A does or says something to B, not *all* responses are open to B. If communication has occurred, what B does is in some way constrained by A's input.

Constraint implies a code imposed on the relationship between A and B, such that each may interpret the other's behavior more or less accurately. Speech, writing, facial expressions, gestures, semaphore, smoke signals, all have served as codes. Because of culturally patterned constraints, people are able to class some perceptions as the same or similar and others as different. All the social sciences are based on this simple but extremely important fact.

SCSs have boundaries, not necessarily geographically contiguous, across which exchanges with the environment occur. For our purposes here, we may consider the environment to include natural habitat and circumjacent SCSs. Because these exchanges with the environment occur, an SCS can be described as an open system. All exchanges between an open system and its environments are dual. Whatever enters the SCS must leave it, at some time or another, whether or not its state has been transformed. This sort of dual exchange may be called a *throughput*, and there are three throughputs of chief concern to us here. The first is that of the units themselves. People enter an SCS and sooner or later leave it. They engage in two kinds of environmental exchanges: first, that of matter and energy, and second, that of information. We may take these one at a time.

INDIVIDUALS

One of the most important properties of individual members of an SCS is progression through time, or aging.

> We find examples of populations—aggregates of individuals conforming to a common definition—in which individuals are added (born) and subtracted (die) and in which the age of the individual is a relevant and identifiable variable. . . Population change, both in absolute numbers and in structure, can be discussed in terms of birth and survival functions relating numbers of births and deaths in specific age groups to various aspects of the system. . . . The interaction of populations can be discussed in terms of competitive, complementary, or parasitic relationships among populations of different species, whether the species consist of animals, commodities, social classes, or molecules [Boulding 1968: 5].

These statements are true even if relatively simple systems are considered. A clock, for example, will not run forever even if it is wound regularly. The parts age and wear away at different rates, and sooner or later some part or set of parts will break down and the system will fail unless the parts are replaced. Aging, failure, and replacement of units is as characteristic of cultures as it is of clocks.

MATTER AND ENERGY

It is assumed that one of the primary functions of tools and other forms of matter is to increase the efficiency of the sociocultural system in terms of the amount of energy harnessed. The problem of harnessing energy has been discussed at length by others (see White 1949; 1959; Sahlins and Service 1960), so we will focus here on the throughput of matter.

The exchange of material with the environment is mediated by technology—the aggregate of tools and techniques directly concerned with livelihood. Technology may be relatively simple, as it is among hunters and gatherers, or extremely complex, as it is among highly industrialized SCSs. Technology is of critical importance in the systemic metaphor because it is an expression of the efficiency of the SCS in adapting to and utilizing its resources. Note that we are discussing the efficiency of the sociocultural system, not the happiness, contentment, or satisfaction of its members.

Like many other complex systems, SCSs exhibit a tendency toward growth, an increase in internal complexity. The rate at which such growth occurs is associated with the complexity of the tools and activities used to exploit the environment. Generally speaking, the greater the technological inventory, the more combinations of items are possible, and the more likely it is that the SCS will be characterized by a high rate of technological growth.

The material input is of two types. First, artifactual input consists of tools, buildings, clothing, and other material goods derived from natural substances which are put to use extraorganismically—that is, outside the bodies of the individual members of the SCS. These goods are used and then discarded, either after they have served their purpose or after they have become so worn that it is easier to replace them than to restore them. With use, different kinds of material pass through an SCS at different rates: A stone building lasts longer than a bamboo hut. Similarly, the same kinds of artifacts pass through different societies at different rates. An alarm clock will last longer when used in a cool, dry climate rather than in a hot, moist one.

The rates at which artifacts pass through an SCS may be referred to as that system's materials attrition rate. As an aside, it may be mentioned that in so-called underdeveloped societies the economic condition is partly a function of the high materials attrition rate. Where artifactual goods are stolen or quickly destroyed by climate, it would be dysfunctional to invest much productive effort in acquiring goods. In Samoa, ripe yellow bananas are high-priced, and banana plants abound, yet Samoans rarely eat a yellow banana. The reason is that the moment anyone's bananas show signs of ripening, they are begged, confiscated, or stolen by someone else. Thus everyone must eat his bananas while they are still green. This is called a leveling mechanism. Such other leveling mechanisms as large feasts, forced loans, and expenditure rivalries, however much they may promote social solidarity, tend to disperse wealth and inhibit its reinvestment (Nash 1966: 35–36). Clearly, the production of material goods depends as much on the cooperation of other members of a sociocultural system as on the motivation of the entrepreneur himself.

It is worthy of note that a high material attrition rate is also characteristic of industrialized societies with relatively unregulated economies, at least for certain types of artifacts. This is true to the extent that manufacturers profit from the sale of artifacts designed to fall apart on schedule. Production is predicated on the assumption that all artifactual goods will break down, and from the point of view of some of the artisans, the sooner the better. Advertising and built-in obsolescence are similarly attempts to maintain a high material attrition rate.

A second type of material input is victual, consisting of food taken from the environment, consumed and converted into energy, and eliminated. As Cohen (1968: 42–43) observes, the nature of victual input yields some indication of the efficiency of the SCS. In many simple and relatively isolated societies, the diet remains monotonously regular throughout the year or shifts abruptly from one season to the next as one kind of food disappears and another becomes available. Conversely, an efficient SCS utilizes trade relationships in such a way that many kinds of food are available regardless of season. A less efficient SCS can make few dietary substitutions, and its welfare is therefore likely to be bound up with the success of a limited number of highly important food sources.

INFORMATION

The term *information* is used here broadly, rather than in any mathematical sense. It may be defined as the syntactical constraint imposed on or developed in any entity as it relates with other entities linked by some communication channel. If communication is to occur, the participants must have corresponding constraints mapped or coded into the system of each (Silverman 1968: 150).

Information may enter the SCS through innovation or through environmental experience. The information may be of varying utility to the SCS. To the extent that it is socially useful or functional, it may be instrumental in the exchange of matter and energy with the environment, or it may be expressive by ideologically justifying a set of subsistence techniques, enhancing solidarity, or otherwise indirectly promoting durability of the SCS.

Information sharing The course of data throughput occurs in this way: new information appears in an SCS and, functional or not, is stored away. In other words, when people learn something new they remember it for a while or they file it away artifactually. The individuals in an SCS then constitute data banks, and these banks are periodically scanned by means of processes varying in degree of formality from gossip and visiting to staff meetings and court trials (see Roberts 1964). Much of the information is also transmitted from one person to another so that it comes to be absorbed into the shared informational inventory.

The extent to which any information is shared varies greatly. At one extreme, the data become what Linton has called a *universal*, absorbed into a core of behavioral predispositions, and it may become so characteristic of fully participating adults in an SCS that everyone knows and expects it. At the other extreme, the data may be shared by only two or three individuals and deliberately kept secret from others. It is said, for example, that the formula for a popular Italian liqueur is not recorded and is known to only three people, and that these three never travel together so that in the event of a fatal accident the formula will not be lost.

There are of course numerous reasons for keeping information secret. Among other things, if two sociocultural systems are in competition, information known to one of them and kept secret from the other will give the knowledgeable SCS a competitive advantage. Even if the actual advantage is slight, suspicion that the competitor controls secret information may make members of the uninformed SCS adopt a more cautious strategy. The same is true for competitive subsystems within a sociocultural system.

Two latent functions of secret information are also apparent. One of these, subsystem differentiation, is analogous to the process called *sharpening* in the psychology of perception. If a subsystem controls information and deliberately keeps it secret from similar subsystems, it sharpens its own boundaries and pulls its members closer together in a conspiracy of silence. This is a prerequisite for the second latent function: enhancement of the self-imagery of subsystem members. Secrecy and value are intimately associated in people's minds.[2] It is not only that valuable information should be kept secret from members of other subsystems, but that what is kept secret is itself an expression of what is valuable. Secret handshakes do not help one fraternity to adapt more efficiently than another, but they do acquire a kind of fiat value as a reflection of the brothers' pride in their organization. There are many examples of such expressive information in the ethnographic literature. C. A. Valentine provides one illustration in his discussion of ritual among the men of the Lakalai of New Britain:

> All the supplementary mystification which surrounds the masks and the performances not only contributes to masculine pride but heightens the atmosphere of secrecy and the sense of the uncanny as well. Sanctity and taboo further intensify these effects. None but the initiated may handle the masks or witness the transformations from ordinary person to masked man.
>
> Yet virtually the only real secrets beneath all this elaborate cultural camouflage are the details of the internal structures of the masks and the procedures surrounding their construction [Valentine 1962: 48].

Goffman makes a similar point: "Often the real secret behind the mystery is that there really is no mystery: the real problem is to prevent the audience from learning this too" (Goffman 1959: 70). And other recent works (see Young 1965) have demonstrated that among the chief functions of secret information are the expression, maintenance, and enhancement of subsystem solidarity.

Storage and control   The simplest means of storing information is by remembering it. In fact, in many SCSs that lack a written language, this is one of the few means available. Under these circumstances, information is exchanged orally in face-to-face encounters. This transmission by human speech is characterized by rapid evanescence, or fading; the sound waves which transmit the message are progressively dampened by environmental noise until they are no longer detectable.

More complicated methods of information storage involve the encoding of the message into a symbolic arrangement of material elements which evanesce more slowly than speech. In writing, for example, one encodes speech into an arbitrary set of symbols (letters, say) and organizes certain materials (pen and ink) in such a way that the information symbolized by the syntax, or arrangement of words, is represented on paper. As long as this arrangement of elements lasts, the information may be read by anyone with access to the same coded constraints the writer is using. This is true of all techniques of artifactual storage. Data are encoded, then the code is imposed on a set of material elements in the form of a stable arrangement of parts, whether the parts be letters on paper, oxide molecules on magnetic tape, or notches on a stick; then the message is retrieved or decoded and put to use.

All stored information involves a stable arrangement of elements; and, conversely, all stable states constitute stored information, in the sense that they are records of past events. Historical geologists, for example, attempt to decode information stored systematically, by nature, in the various layers of the earth's crust. Similarly, in some geographical areas archeologists can use dendrochronological techniques based on information stored in the growth rings of tree trunks. All such interpretations of nonrandom arrangements depend upon our ability to determine the constraints imposed by one event upon a succeeding one.

Even without artifactual storage, the amount of information in any given SCS is likely to be more than the sum of the information controlled by any individual members. The pieces of information controlled by individuals often fit together like pieces of a jigsaw puzzle. Each worker on an assembly line may know only enough to perform his limited task, but together the workers constitute a production unit.

One of the more obvious consequences of elaborate techniques for the artifactual storage of information is that the individual himself becomes less important as a storage "cell." In relatively primitive societies one of the functions of old people is to remember legends, myths, and ethical principles, and they are frequently consulted on these matters. Elliott (1886: 170–171) described the situation among the Aleuts, neighbors of the Eskimo in the northern Pacific:

Before the advent of Russian priests, every village had one or two old men at least, who considered it their especial business to educate the children; thereupon, in the morning or the evening, when all were at home, these aged teachers would seat themselves in the center of one of the largest village courts or "oolagmuh": the young folks surrounded them, and listened attentively to what they said—sometimes failing memory would cause the old preceptors to repeat over and over again the same advice or legend in the course of a lecture. The respect of the children, however, never allowed or occasioned an interruption of such a senile oration.

Such were the conditions in at least one nonliterate society a century ago. A further perusal of the ethnographic literature suggests the proposition that when writing appears among a people characterized by a low rate of literacy, and when books and other archives are rare, artifactual storage of information does not necessarily replace the oldsters; rather, it supplements their memories. Usually the first written records to appear in a predominantly nonliterate society are sacred writings and reports of economic transactions. As a rule, access to these archives is controlled by a class of specially educated persons, who may or may not be priests, and who are older than the general population. The members of this educated class then transmit such information to lay people as they deem wise.

This sort of arrangement persisted in Europe until almost 500 years ago when, with the spread of the printing press, esoteric information became generally available. This, in fact, suggests the origin of the university lecture system, developed at a time when books were copied by hand and so rare that they were read aloud before the class by professor–priests.

In industrialized societies, the mythology that remains important to the SCS is written down, printed, and sold in bookstores. The world's best seller is the Bible; more than 1.5 billion copies have appeared since 1800, in 1,280 languages. Such improved storage devices may render older people redundant as consultants and arbitrators.[3]

Scanning procedures retrieve and apply relevant information. Information that is not useful disappears from a system rapidly, either because the people who knew it forgot it, or because they die. Given enough time and enough change in an SCS, all data eventually become useless and disappear from the system. These processes of storing, scanning, and retrieving information are examined in a paper by Roberts (1964), which applies the concepts to an analysis of the political development of several American Indian societies.

The criteria by which information is judged socially useful or functional are the quantity and nature of the material and energy input of the system, the technology that affects it, the expressive information that facilitates it, and the cumulative impact of these subsistence-related activities on the relationships between component subsystems.

In principle, it might be said, all the information that any system could possibly use is being transmitted from the environment. The kind and amount of "absolute information" (Brillouin 1968: 162) received, however, is determined by the arrangement of the SCS parts. This arrangement of parts generates a distinctive external orientation, or set of constraints, within the SCS.

It is worth suggesting that the existence of people who have information that is of little value to others may contribute to the overall adaptability of any SCS, because currently worthless information may someday become useful as the SCS changes. To the extent that an SCS lacks nonfunctional information, it resembles a highly specialized organism which depends for maximal efficiency on a specific configuration of environmental elements.[4]

The existence of people whose knowledge is of little or no utility to other SCS members means that the SCS is still generalized to a degree and that, should there be a drastic alteration in rate or direction of SCS change, the knowledge they control may mean the difference between survival and extinction for the total system. At the same time, while it is true that previously nonfunctional knowledge may become functional, it is perhaps less likely that knowledge rendered nonfunctional may ever regain its previous value. Information related to obsolete occupational skills, for example, will probably remain nonfunctional, and it is unfortunate for the aged that they so often act as storage units for this sort of information.

Matching of inputs and SCS components From a conceptual perspective, information storage units are not individuals but rather the roles enacted by individuals. This occurs because the informational inventory consists of that knowledge to which members of an SCS have access, either directly (by remembering it) or indirectly (by scanning data banks). Access to information and the capacity to process that information are functions of the roles people play. Indeed, it is possible to disregard the role structure too, and an approach has been developed by Roberts (1951; 1956; 1961; 1964) which views as information all of what is usually defined as culture.

All extant SCSs are in a constant state of change, so it is not possible to assume that any given system is in a steady state. We may nevertheless assume that there is at least a modicum of congruence in the nature of the three inputs. That is to say, the structure of roles formed by individuals within the SCS must involve storage of such information as will enable the system as a whole to adapt to external circumstances, maintain the throughput of material and energy, and survive. From the point of view of individuals, this means that they must learn enough of the right kinds of information to enable them to make a living and get along with neighbors and kinsmen in their given sociocultural context.

AGING

Let us assume that our individual personalities reflect the information we have acquired so far in our lives and that the most influential and enduring information was acquired in the years leading to maturity. The validity of this proposition is debatable—certainly learning occurs throughout life—but it is commonly accepted in the behavioral sciences, and it certainly seems true of many kinds of animals as well. Zoo keepers tell us that you can't teach an old dog new tricks; and you can't teach an old lion either. As Hediger (1964: 27) observed in the case of captured wild animals:

> The transplanted animal's behavior may be of two different kinds, depending on its origin or the new locality. The second kind is usually seen in the undeveloped still adaptable young wild animal; it may fit the new environment and settle down to it. The first kind on the other hand occurs with the older wild animal already set in its ways and rigidly conditioned by its previous background. It has lost its plasticity and adaptability, and so must behave as it always has done. True, such individuals may often be kept in captivity for a time, but they never become properly adapted to the new situation. If they survive capture they usually linger in a chronic state of excitement generally caused by their uneasiness in the presence of man, and with a basically rigid attitude of mind, so to speak. This prevents any suitable treatment, even the taking of food; it may result in nervous disturbances [and] reduce resistance to disease and [may] lead to death, psychologically caused.

The existence of such a response to change among human beings has also received some empirical support (Lieberman 1961; Camargo and Preston 1945). On the whole, the aged tend to be the more stable and conservative members of any SCS. Of course, it is not necessarily true that they become more conservative as they change through time, but they may stay pretty much the same while the SCS changes, or they may change more slowly. This is probably not merely a contemporary phenomenon. Two thousand years ago,

Plato was complaining about the recklessness and disobedience of the young.

Around the world, the aged seem to be the guardians of the old traditions. Alland (1967: 219) calls this the result of "learning fixation" while Riley and Foner (1968: 5) summarize a number of recent findings in this way: "In general, older people are more conservative than younger people in their political ideology. . . . Age appears to contribute for better or for worse, to the stability of the social structure."

Given these assumptions, we have then a situation in which old people die in an SCS and new ones are born and replace them. These young people in turn grow up, learning as they grow, until they become fully participating adults, displaying relatively fixed values and behavioral predispositions. Gradually they too become old and die. Their death is actually an essential part of social life, as was the death of the aged persons they replaced. Aside from the problem of population control, there are other difficulties in managing too long-lived a population. Boulding (1970) describes one of them this way: "[Immortality] . . . would present the human race with probably the greatest crisis it has ever had to face. Who, for instance, would want to be an assistant professor for 500 years? What makes life tolerable, especially for the young, is death."

Then too, if the behavior of older persons is relatively conservative and fixed, the replacement of old people by changeable young enhances the adaptability of the SCS and thus increases its chances for survival.

It is clear that the information we acquire during our youthful years will remain useful for the remainder of our lives if there is little or no change in the environment of our SCS. If nothing else changes, learning that was initially useful goes on being useful no matter how old we become.

On the other hand, as the environment changes, the slower-changing information controlled by the older individual becomes less adaptive to the SCS and ultimately becomes nonfunctional. A high rate of environmental change generates a high rate of sociocultural change because the SCS tends to adapt and survive. Faced with a highly mutative technology and set of values, the older person clings to those skills and beliefs he learned in his youth. In other words, as part of the total system, older persons represent banks of potentially useless data; and the information they control, whether instrumental or expressive, may be of little utility to the rest of society. The congruence between what they know and what the SCS needs to know in order to adapt is highly likely to decline during their lifetime.

Over time, all systems as complex as an SCS tend to maximize the storage and retrieval of socially useful information. This is because rewards ordinarily accrue to people whose function it is to keep the SCS adaptive by controlling and applying socially useful information. In other words, the man who has shown that he knows how to hunt successfully and the shaman who has shown that he knows how to treat disease are likely to be better off than the unskilled hunter or the unpracticed shaman. The aged and any others whose information is of little utility tend not to be rewarded. And as their material welfare declines, they develop a parasitic relationship with the other members of the SCS.

It may be argued that many aged and infirm people are well provided for by their children, even in societies characterized by a high rate of institutional change. They may be shown a great deal of respect, so that this generalization lacks credibility. Children may support their parents, whether the parents know anything of value or not. It can be pointed out, however, that within the context of the family—which is a subsystem of the total SCS—aged persons may control information that is socially useful in the *expressive* sense. They may repeat anecdotes about family ancestors, explain kinship networks, serve as instructors in ritual esoterica, and in other ways contribute information that lends historical depth to the family and enhances its survival as a corporate unit.

The situation that is historically normal in industrialized SCSs, of course, is that only the aged, who control obsolete information, and the young, who do not control enough exploitable information, are devalued. But it is possible to imagine an SCS in which the rate of institutional change is so rapid that not only the information controlled by the aged is quickly rendered unexploitable, but also the information controlled by the fully participating adults. One requirement of social life is that there be continuity enough in the demands of the role structure to permit people to be prepared for and recruited into appropriate roles.

In terms more consistent with the systemic model we have been using, we might point out that as the amount and rate of information input are increased, errors increase too, until the channel capacity of the system is exceeded. From our own experience we know that it is easy to drive a car along a country road, where we can easily handle the few novel circumstances that arise. We know also that it seems to take more energy to drive through city traffic or on a crowded freeway, where the rate and kinds of novel information input are great, and where we are more likely to make a driving error. And we can imagine a situation—for example, on a first visit in a foreign country—in which we are surrounded by vehicles moving quickly and erratically. In such a situation we might not be able to drive at all because we would be unable to receive and process all the novel information with which we were being bombarded.

There is no reason to suppose that SCSs are not subject to comparable limits. Margaret Mead's second study of the village of Pere (1956) suggests that some of these limits may be broader than we have thought, and that some SCSs can adapt to changing circumstances rather readily. On the other hand, we have the experience of many segments of American Indian society, which were bombarded with environmental change at such a rapid rate that the established adaptive mechanisms of the society were unable to handle it. Thus the SCS itself lost its integrative quality, and the population failed to reproduce itself (see Bohannan and Plog 1967).

At the other end of the continuum of SCS change rates, we might imagine a society in which the rate of change was insignificant. Ideally, assuming that individuals accumulate useful information step by step throughout their lives and therefore know more with each passing year, then all other things being equal, the person of most value to the society would be the one who had lived the longest. If the control of socially useful information were associated with political power, a gerontocracy might result.

The preceding statements suggest some of the reasons why the aged are generally devalued in industrialized SCSs, which are characterized by rapid change and by elaborate means of artifactual information storage.

It should not be thought, incidentally, that in referring to industrialized SCSs, we mean to include only those which are socially complex; that is, those with a high population density, cities of considerable size, a complicated division of labor, and so forth. The operative concept here is the substitution of machines for men in subsistence-getting activities. The rate of institutional change may be significantly different in complex societies with peasant-based economies and in the industrialized societies of Europe and North America. Far too little quantitative comparison has been made in the area. For example, Kalish (1969: 85) asked a group of about two dozen Cambodian students, coming from a complex but largely agrarian society, whether:

> given the necessity of choice, they would save the life of their mother, their wife, or their daughter. All responded immediately that they would save their mother, and their tone implied that only an immoral or ignorant person would even ask such a question. [Kalish doubts] whether 10% of a comparable American group would give that response.

Kastenbaum (1964) asked a group of American nurses how much effort they would expend in saving the lives of a twenty-year-old, an eighty-year-old, and a pet dog. The results showed that the lives were ranked in an expectable order of importance—twenty-year-old, eighty-year-old, and pet dog—but it is noteworthy that the difference between the twenty-year-old and the eighty-year-old was greater than the difference between the eighty-year-old and the dog.

Of course, a high rate of change in a sociocultural system is not the only condition under which the aged may be treated poorly. Devaluation can occur under other conditions as well. In industrialized SCSs we see it because the older person is not able to change the information he controls rapidly enough to keep up with the changing needs of the SCS. However, among certain hunting and gathering societies, characterized by simple technology and enforced geographic mobility under harsh environmental circumstances, it may occur simply because the older person is not able physically to keep up with the others as they move around in their search for food. Such conditions are found by Holmberg (1969: 224–225) among the Siriono of the Bolivian rain forest, for example.

> Since status is determined largely by immediate utility to the group, the inability of the aged to compete with the younger members of the society places them somewhat in the category of excess baggage. Having outlived their usefulness they are relegated to a position of obscurity. Actually the aged are quite a burden. They eat but are unable to hunt, fish, or collect food; they sometimes hoard a young spouse, but are unable to beget children; they move at a snail's pace and hinder the mobility of the group. . . . When a person becomes too ill or infirm to follow the fortunes of the band, he is abandoned to shift for himself.

To put this in other terms, the ecological adjustment of some SCS is such that the people must travel about frequently or rapidly in order to secure food and drink enough for survival. Here, if the SCS changes little, the aged may control useful information. However, if much of this information is shared by others, the aged become redundant and may be physically sacrificed because they hamper the quest of their fellows for food or water.

It is important to understand that redundancy alone does not lead to abandonment or sacrifice. A certain amount of redundancy or repetition is functional in a communication system because it reduces the likelihood of transmission error and inadvertent loss. Rather, the redundancy of the aged makes their abandonment possible, but redundancy alone is by no means a sufficient cause. It should also be pointed out that these generalizations apply to some hunting and gathering societies, but others have considerable leisure time and ample food for their unproductive oldsters (Lee and DeVore 1968; Lee 1969). One may assume that the killing or abandonment of the aged occurs in societies where they are dealt with contemptuously. This is not necessarily the case, as we shall see.

In any event, one may note a paradoxical effect here. In relatively simple societies under relatively harsh environmental conditions, the rate of SCS change and the tempo of informational obsolescence may be low, but integration into society depends a great deal on physical strength, or at least endurance, of which the aged have little. In other words, they may control useful information but are not strong enough to adapt to the demands of their surroundings. In industrialized societies, on the other hand, more efficient tools and a more complex division of labor make work less dependent on physical strength; but a highly developed technology means a high rate of SCS change, so that the elderly become more or less rapidly obsolete as parts of the man–machine system.

SUMMARY

We know that the status and treatment of the aged vary greatly from one society to another. In those societies where they are killed or abandoned, as among some hunters and gatherers, the aged may or may not have relatively high status up to the point of death. On the other hand, we have suggested that where SCS change is rapid, because the society is undergoing or had undergone industrialization, or because of culture contact with a more dominant, complex society, the information controlled by the aged becomes rapidly obsolete. This high rate of informational obsolescence is reflected in a decline in the social participation of the elderly. The low incidence of social participation in turn contributes to their loss of status.

More specifically, we propose that societies may be ranked in terms of the participation of their aged members in social life. (This participation is of course made possible by their control of useful information.) It is also proposed that societies may be ranked in terms of the status accorded to their aged. Finally, it is hypothesized that, inasmuch as a person is socially valuable largely because of his knowledge, the status of the aged should vary directly with their participation in the social life of the community.

Methods and Results

It remains for us to give some empirical substance to the general propositions presented in the foregoing discussion. Attempting to build on the efforts of Simmons, we made use of the Human Relations Area Files (HRAF). The HRAF is a collection of ethnographic materials already coded into such categories as "dancing," "visiting and hospitality," and "community structure," among others. This information is coded separately for each of the nearly 200 societies in the HRAF, an arrangement which greatly facilitates cross-cultural research. But because of the inherent limitations of the HRAF as a research tool, various constraints were imposed on the hypotheses that could be formulated and the procedures that could be employed in the analysis of the data.

This is not the place to deal with the technical complexities of large-scale cross-cultural research. With varying success in wrestling with the many difficulties, a considerable literature in comparative methodology already exists, not only in anthropology but in several related disciplines.[5] It should be mentioned, however, that the problem is compounded in the present instance because of the previously mentioned paucity of data on the aged in the ethnographic corpus. Thus this initial attempt is more a pilot study than a definitive work with adequate sampling procedures and carefully defined units of analysis.

The systems-theoretical approach adopted here requires that the aged be viewed as one of several subsets in an SCS which is capable, in varying degrees, of receiving, processing, and transmitting information. It is further proposed that any understanding of the treatment of the aged must take into account the internal arrangement of informational resources available to a particular SCS. Our previous discussion has indicated some of the conditions which affect the role of the aged as sources of information for the larger society. Our problem now is to specify how this position of the elderly determines the kind of treatment they receive within the system as a whole.

The hypothesis to be tested states that the esteem in which the aged are held in a given society varies directly with the control they maintain over the society's informational resources. By esteem we refer to the society's treatment of the aged insofar as this treatment maintains the integrity and worth of the aged as a subset of the SCS. Although the precise operational definition is somewhat problematical, it seems clear that the aged are recognized in all SCSs as a distinct category (see Linton 1942). Thus each SCS must make some choice as to the manner in which it will deal with the aged as a social configuration, from veneration at one extreme to contempt at the other.

The independent variable of information control refers to the amount of information processed by the aged, relative to the total informational pool available to the SCS. Before focusing on the operational details of our attempt to measure this variable, it is necessary to state the general methodological procedures used in this study.

After perusing the data available in the HRAF, it was decided that the most productive way to proceed was to use as a sample all the societies for which relatively detailed descriptive data were filed under the categories relevant to the treatment of the aged. Using the files housed at City University of New York, coders collected data from a pool of some thirty societies. Protocols were developed on four variables: (1) information control among the aged, (2) treatment of the aged, (3) rate of institutional change, and (4) ecological factors affecting the aged. The last two variables are not treated systematically here, but attempts have been made to deal with these and certain other variables, such as power, in a more extensive examination of this general problem (Maxwell and Silverman 1971; Silverman and Maxwell 1971; and Silverman and Maxwell 1972).

From the original pool of thirty societies, protocols were completed for twenty-six cases. This sample is distributed geographically over the major ethnographic areas of the world: East Eurasia,· 8; North America, 6; Africa, 4; Circum-Mediterranean, 4; Insular Pacific, 2; and South America, 2. Furthermore, no two cases share the sampling provinces specified by Murdock (1968). Lastly, the sample covers a variety of cultural types, including hunters and gatherers, pastoralists, horticulturalists, peasants, and several societies with a mixed economic base.

With respect to the independent variable, information control, data were coded on the role played by the aged in social situations along two dimensions. First, each instance was coded for the relevant aspect of culture content involved, such as political, economic, or ideological. Second, and more important for our purpose, each instance was coded for one of five informational processes involving the aged in terms of (1) participating in situations, such as feasts, games, or visiting groups; (2) consulting; (3) making decisions; (4) entertaining; or (5) arbitrating. Before the coding procedures had gotten far, it was found necessary to add a sixth category: teaching. It can be demonstrated that these informational process categories form a unidimensional variable of increasing elaboration, thus this pool of six items may reasonably be considered a measure of information control available to the aged.

Using the sample of twenty-six societies, an attempt was made to construct a Guttman scale for both dimensions of the information control variable.[6] Whiting, one of the most knowledgeable anthropologists in the area of cross-cultural studies, has judged the scaling of cultural features the best method of measurement in comparative research (1968: 714). Of course, not all data can be subjected to this sort of scrutiny and then ordered. For example, various scaling procedures were applied to the first dimension of information control—content categories—but no reasonable pattern could be constructed among the various aspects of culture. More information seems to be required before such concepts as politics, religion, and economics can be related to the function of the aged within a comparative framework.

Nevertheless, the dimension of informational process proved appropriate for the unidimensional, cumulative ordering inherent in Guttman type scaling. Tables 2–1 and 2–2 present the scalogram and scale developed from the six items of informational process. A score of 1 indicates presence of the item; 0 stands for the absence of an item; and X stands for an error in the scale type. The coefficient of scalability, as developed by Menzel (1953), was used in preference to the coefficient of reproducibility because the former corrects for extreme marginals. Since the measure is more demanding, it tends to produce weaker values than would be obtained with the coefficient of reproducibility. In this case the scale attains a value of .74, which is

Table 2-1 SCALOGRAM OF INFORMATIONAL CONTROL AMONG THE AGED

	1	2	3	4	5	6
I. Bali	1	1	1	1	1	1
Bushmen	1	1	1	1	1	1
Monguor	1	1	1	1	1	1
Ainu	1	1	1	1	1	1
China	1	1	1	X	1	1
Rural Irish	1	1	1	1	X	1
Navaho	1	1	X	1	A	1
II. Korea	1	1	1	1	1	0
Tiv	1	1	1	1	1	0
Kikuyu	1	1	1	X	1	0
III. Chukchee	1	1	1	1	0	0
Gond	1	1	X	1	0	0
Mandan	1	1	X	1	0	0
Ifugao	1	1	X	1	0	0
IV. Tallensi	1	1	1	0	0	0
Serbs	1	1	1	0	0	0
Lapps	1	1	1	0	0	0
Ojibwa	1	1	1	0	0	0
Micmac	1	1	1	0	0	0
Inca	1	1	1	0	0	X
V. Gilyak	1	1	0	0	0	0
Siriono	X	1	0	0	0	0
VI. Rewala	1	0	0	0	0	0
Nahane (Kaska)	1	0	0	0	0	0
Western Tibet	1	0	0	0	X	0
Aleut	1	0	0	0	0	X

Total N = 26; Coefficient of Scalability = .74

reasonably above the suggested level of acceptance, somewhere between .60 and .65.

One somewhat surprising result is that entertaining proved to be a higher scale step than arbitrating. It could well be that not sufficient attention has been given to entertainment as a way of processing information in an SCS. Certainly, it is noteworthy that in a recent national survey among American high school students, Bob Hope is among the top three individuals most admired! With few exceptions, such as Freud's work on joking and various papers on games by Roberts and his associates (for example, Roberts and Sutton-Smith 1962), this dimension of cultural content has been sadly

Table 2-2 SCALE OF INFORMATIONAL CONTROL
AMONG THE AGED

Category	Informational Process	Proportion of Sample Discriminated	Errors*
1	Participating	100	1
2	Consulting	84	0
3	Decision making	77	4
4	Entertaining	54	2
5	Arbitrating	38	3
6	Teaching	27	2

*The error column represents instances of nonscalable responses that may suggest the invalidity of the one scale hypothesis. High frequencies of errors may also suggest alternative hypotheses for the observed relations between the variables.

neglected. Our data suggest that entertainment requires greater, consideration.

The dependent variable in our hypothesis is the treatment of the aged. In order to tap the empirical richness of this variable, a protocol with twenty-four items was used by coders to extract as much of the behavioral diversity as possible. This included such items (all with reference to the aged) as: special place or sitting arrangements; geographical separation; food privileges; special costumes, ornamentation, or body marks; deferential greetings, whether verbal or gestural; exclusive decoration or grooming by others; generalized fear and avoidance by others; abandonment to the elements/animals; and physically assaulted and killed, or sacrificed. Most of the items had either a positive or a negative valence with respect to the integrity of the aged; a few items could have had either valence depending on the context in which they occurred. (A more sophisticated version of this scale is described in Silverman and Maxwell 1975.)

Because the treatment of the aged variable does not lend itself to the more demanding Guttman scaling technique, an alternative procedure was based on a ratio of the positive and negative items available on the protocols. Thus, for each of the 24 items for which it was possible to have information, each code was judged to be either positive (reflecting the high esteem in which the aged are held) or negative (reflecting disdain for the aged). A score was then obtained by subtracting the negative items from the positive ones and dividing by the total number of items, in this case twenty-four.

Of course, the data available on each society did not yield

information on all twenty-four items. Because of the influence of this factor on the rating technique, societies which are poorly reported, and thus have fewer items coded, tend to have slightly deflated scores. Nevertheless, this technique proved to be the most realistic solution to the knotty problem of the discrepancy in the amount of data available for analysis. Since all the societies in the sample were considered to have relatively thorough coverage of the aged, it is somewhat more probable that if the item were present it would have been reported by the ethnographer.

The rating scale for the treatment of the aged is shown in Table 2-3. The higher the score, the greater the esteem enjoyed by the aged. For the purpose of subsequent calculations, the scale is arbitrarily divided into seven numerically equal segments—except for the extremes, where a somewhat broader range of scores is collapsed together.

The distribution of societies in Table 2-3 confirms the proposition discussed earlier which states the conditions under which the aged are devalued. Taking into account only the bottom three levels of the scale, 80 percent of the societies are nomadic during at least part of the annual cycle. On the other hand, only one case among the top four levels of the scale is a nomadic society. The aged among the Bushmen enjoy a very high esteem despite the society's continually moving about, seeking sustenance from the inhospitable Kalahari Desert. Furthermore, this high level of esteem continues to

Table 2-3 SCALE OF TREATMENT OF THE AGED

Culture	Score	Culture	Score
I. China	.79	V. Tiv	.16
Bushmen	.62	Lapps	.16
Monguor	.62	Chukchee	.12
Navaho	.50	Ojibwa	.12
		Gilyak	.12
II. Bali	.42	VI. Korea	.08
		Gond	.08
		Aleut	.08
III. Ainu	.33	Mandan	.04
Rural Irish	.33	Micmac	.04
Tallensi	.33	Rewala	.04
		VII. Siriono	.00
IV. Serbs	.29	Ifugao	−.04
Inca	.25	Western Tibet	−.12
Kikuyu	.20	Nahane (Kaska)	−.12

operate even though those aged who are unable to keep up with the group must occasionally be abandoned.

Although it is true that, with the exception of the Bushmen, all the societies in our sample that abandon and/or assault and kill their aged also score in the lower half of the scale, Koty (1933) provides ample evidence that these extreme measures are not necessarily associated with low esteem. Indeed, of the five cases in our sample where the aged are physically assaulted and killed—among the Chukchee, Lapps, Ojibwa, Ifugao, and Micmac—there is clear evidence in at least the first three cases that this measure is taken only when requested by the elderly victim. Given the scale distribution of societies where such extreme treatment categories are found, our measure of esteem appeared sensitive enough to take account of these ethnographic facts.

It is now possible to consider the test of the hypothesis regarding the relationship between informational control and the treatment of the aged. The data from Tables 2–1 and 2–3 were used to calculate a measure of association. It is worth noting that each of these scales was constructed by judges working independently of each other, thus avoiding one possible source of contamination. The measure of association used to relate the two scales is the Gamma coefficient, which has been judged to be the most easily interpretable for the analysis of ordinal scale data.[7] The correlation of the two scales attains a Gamma value of .685 ($p < .01$), thus giving relatively strong support for the hypothesis that the control of various informational processes among the aged will predict the degree of esteem they enjoy within a particular society.

Discussion

First of all, we developed a scale of informational control among the aged people of twenty-six societies from the many societies available in the HRAF. The six items of the scale were found to be unidimensional, with the items running from most common to least common: (1) participating in social situations; (2) consulting; (3) decision making; (4) entertaining; (5) arbitrating; and (6) teaching. Second, we scored each of the twenty-six societies for treatment of their aged, based on the presence or absence of twenty-four traits dealing with the behavior of other members of the SCS toward old people. (Expectedly, China was at the top of the positive end.) Finally, we demonstrated an association between the two scales which, within the limits of the experimental design and procedures, seems to indicate that control over useful information does determine to some extent the treatment of the aged in the SCS.

The last finding, that high informational control among the aged is associated with their being held in esteem, will startle few who are familiar with previous cross-cultural efforts. This, after all, is part of the import of Simmons's book. Generalizing from his perusal of the literature, he states:

> Even though the aged have had to withdraw from the rigors of life and betake themselves to domestic shelter, they have not been entirely doomed to passivity. The aged have not been mere social parasites. By the exercise of their knowledge, wisdom, experience, property rights, and religious or magical powers they have often played useful roles [1945: 216].

Such a brief treatment of the subject as we have presented here raises more issues than it resolves. We will make seven problems explicit in unordered fashion.

It became clear in the course of this preliminary investigation that Simmons was right; there were indeed vast differences in the treatment of the aged according to sex. But his suggested determinant, the organization of the family, is not really satisfactory for several reasons. If it is true that old men have relatively higher status in strongly patrilineal or generally male-oriented societies like the Chinese, and conversely, if old women are held in relatively high esteem in matrilineal or female-oriented societies like the Navaho, there is nevertheless reason to wonder why some societies are patrilineal and others matrilineal in the first place. Moreover, a case could be made for strong lineality being a *result* of differential esteem, rather than a cause.

The comment that correlations do not prove causality could be made of this paper or, in fact, almost any other synchronic, comparative study, though in the present case perhaps with somewhat less force. Dealing as one does with the static, descriptive data of HRAF, it is difficult to demonstrate the direction of causality. Yet it is not impossible if, for example, one is able to trace the thread back to climatic variables (see Whiting 1964; Maxwell 1967) or if one adopts certain logicostatistical techniques suggested by Blalock (1964). Alternatively, of course, if complete historical data were available for a number of societies, one might then establish the temporal sequence of changes in the independent and dependent variables.

In a similar vein, we feel that the correlation presented earlier between information control and exteem has not gone far enough. We have suggested that rapid institutional change, which is characteristic of industrialized SCSs as well as others in situations of intense culture contact, generates a high rate of informational obsolescence and thus leads to the devaluation of the aged. The link between rapid SCS change and loss of information control for the aged remains to be demonstrated.

In association with the tempo of SCS change, certain other factors undoubtedly assert themselves. In SCSs such as the United States, the rapidity of SCS change seems to result in part from the complexity of the informational inventory. The more items in the inventory, the more combinations are possible and the more likely they are to be made. On the other hand, what are generally called *ecological variables* are obviously at work in our own society as well as others. Population density, availability of resources, climate, ease of transport, community locations favorable or inimical to trade with other peoples—all are important determinants of the tempo of SCS change. And these are all aside from the direct impact of the environment on the ability of a population to support unproductive old people.

The limits of the social category "old person" vary greatly from place to place. In some societies a man may be considered old when he becomes a grandfather, which may be in his fortieth year. Or the ethnographer himself may be the judge of who is old and who is not. And we have not drawn any distinction in this study between people who are merely old and people who are decrepit. This is not because the distinction is unimportant, but because it is so seldom made in the ethnographic literature. It would be informative to consider the position of the decrepit in, say, a society in which old people are held in great esteem.

On the one hand, the response of the other SCS members is subject to generalization from more powerful and respected elders to their disoriented and enfeebled fellows. On the other hand, if it is true, as we have suggested, that esteem is determined by control of socially useful information, then the decrepit aged are indeed socially bankrupt. The balance between the two forces must be a delicate one. And, if we are thinking in terms of something like compassion toward the aged, the truly decrepit provide a more critical test of compassion than the merely old.

During the investigation it was apparent that the content categories of information control—political, economic, social, religious, and so on—could not be subjected to unidimensional scaling, but the distinction in each category between instrumental and expressive information was of little importance. The relationship of the variables appears to hold regardless of whether information being processed is instrumental or expressive. This is certainly a point worth pursuing in future research.

A final observation is that the model presented here is really too simple. We have already discussed the importance of ecological factors and the rate of institutional change in the SCS. In addition, other informational variables should certainly be taken into account as possible intervening factors affecting the predicted relationship. We may mention one such consideration: linguistic homogeneity–heterogeneity. Like Russian and Spanish, the English language is relatively homogeneous. It is bifurcated only into Commonwealth or North American dialects. Other languages, like Chinese, are made up of several mutually nearly unintelligible dialects. And at the other extreme, as in some parts of Africa, dialects may be separated only by a few villages. Linguistic heterogeneity–homogeneity is of enormous importance for trade, transport, solidarity, and other aspects of social and economic relationships, as well as for the deliberate exchange of socially useful information! However, it is not at all clear how or if this variable is related to the treatment of old people. Doubtless other such informational variables are yet to be considered or even recognized in sociocultural gerontology.

These theoretical and methodological points have been brought up here not in order to vitiate the results of the present study but rather to delineate some problem areas for further research. Indeed, the findings presented here represent only part of the data collected from HRAF, and we expect to devote more attention to these and other problems in the future. Crossnational studies of aging have been facilitated by the existence of archives, even though the large-scale cross-cultural approach that takes into account primitive as well as technologically advanced societies has in the past been hampered by skimpy or uneven data.

In practical matters there is an ongoing diffusion of effective medical care as well as the increasing incorporation of simple societies within nation-state systems. Perhaps these will make the cross-cultural study of aging somewhat more significant as a heuristic technique. The United States is, after all, but one of many thousands of societies in the world. And each society is in a sense a self-contained experiment in the handling of older people. Each is searching for a solution to a social problem that all face.

Notes

1. Koty (1933) attempted to cover the ethnographic literature on the treatment of the aged and the sick before such data banks as the Human Relations Area Files made comparative research a more manageable task. Although his theoretical perspective is outdated, the book contains much useful information, particularly from Russian sources.

2. The valence of secret information may of course be negative as well as positive in that, if it were generally known, it would discredit the subsystem. Goffman (1963: chapter 2) discusses techniques of controlling such information.

3. In the course of his field work among the Lozi of Zambia, Philip Silverman (1968) queried one of his informants concerning certain aspects of indigenous law. The reply of the informant was a sort of verbal shrug and a statement to the effect that the Lozi no longer needed to worry about remembering these traditions because it was now all written down for them. "It's all in here," he said, producing a book, *The Judicial Process Among the Barotse*, written years earlier by the anthropologist Max Gluckman, who had been Silverman's colleague at the University of Manchester.

4. Similar generalizations were expressed by Sahlins and Service (1960) as the "law of evolutionary potential," and by Ashby (1956) as the "law of requisite variety." For example, a specialized system is highly adapted to a given environment; it can do only one kind of thing, essentially, but it does it extremely well. However, in a generalized system little adaptation has taken place; many functionally useless elements may be contained within it. Compared to more specialized systems, it is inefficient and sloppy.

5. A good overview of the main methodological problems can be obtained from Whiting (1968).

6. In Guttman scaling, analysis is focused on whether a set of respondents (societies in this study) and a set of items (informational processes involving the aged) can be logically ordered together on a scale in terms of a property (information control) described in variable degree in the items and invoked in variable degree by the respondents when they decide to accept or reject each item. Ideally, both the set of items and the set of respondents are randomly selected. A set of respondents and a set of items are said to be scalable in the Guttman sense when all respondents in the set invoke the same criterion property, albeit in different amounts, in deciding whether to accept or reject each item in the set. (For a more detailed discussion, see Blalock and Blalock 1968: 98–108.)

7. See Costner (1965). In this article, Costner shows that Gamma better meets the requirements as a measure of association if the criterion is the "proportional reduction in error of estimation" made possible by the relationship. Gamma fulfills this criterion better than other rank correlation methods, such as Kendall's Tau and Spearman's Rho. ·

References

Alland, A. *Evolution and Human Behavior.* Garden City, N.Y.: Natural History Press, 1967.

Arensberg, C. M., and S. T. Kimball. *Family and Community in Ireland.* Cambridge: Harvard University Press, 1940.

Ashby, W. R. *An Introduction to Cybernetics*. London: Chapman and Hall, 1956.

Blalock, H. M. *Causal Inferences in Non-experimental Research*. Chapel Hill: University of North Carolina Press, 1964.

———, and Ann B. Blalock, eds. *Methodology in Social Research*. New York: McGraw-Hill, 1968.

Bohannan, P., and F. Plog. *Beyond the Frontier*. Garden City, N.Y.: Natural History Press, 1967.

Boulding, K. E. "General Systems Theory—The Skeleton of a Science." In W. Buckley, ed. *Modern Systems Research for the Behavioral Scientist*. Chicago: Aldine, 1968.

———. "Ecology and Environment." In I. Morrisset and W. W. Stevens, Jr., eds. *Social Science in the Schools: A Search for a Rationale*. New York: Holt, Rinehart and Winston, 1970.

Brillouin, L. "Thermodynamics and Information Theory." In W. Buckley, ed. *Modern Systems Research for the Behavioral Scientist*. Chicago: Aldine, 1968.

Bromley, D. *The Psychology of Human Aging*. Harmondsworth: Penguin, 1966.

Camargo, O., and G. H. Preston. "What Happens to Patients Who Are Hospitalized for the First Time When Over Sixty-five Years of Age." *American Journal of Psychiatry* 102 (1945), 168–173.

Clark, M., and B. G. Anderson. *Culture and Aging*. Springfield, Ill.: Thomas, 1967.

Cohen, Y. A. "Culture as Adaptation." In *Man in Adaptation: The Cultural Present*. Chicago: Aldine, 1968.

Costner, H. L. "Criteria for Measures of Association." *American Sociological Review* 30 (1965), 341–353.

Cowgill, D. O. "Social Life of the Aging in Thailand." Paper presented at annual meeting of the Gerontological Society, Los Angeles, 1965.

———, and L. D. Holmes, eds. *Aging and Modernization*. New York: Appleton–Century–Crofts, 1972.

Elliott, H. W. *Our Arctic Province: Alaska and the Seal Islands*. New York: Scribner's, 1886.

Elwin, V. *The Muria Gond and Their Ghotul*. Bombay: Oxford University Press, 1947.

Goffman, E. *The Presentation of Self in Everyday Life*. Garden City, N.Y.: Doubleday-Anchor, 1959.

———. *Stigma: Notes on the Management of Spoiled Identity*. Englewood Cliffs, N.J.: Prentice-Hall, 1963.

Hart, C. W. M., and A. R. Pilling. *The Tiwi of North Australia*. New York: Holt, Rinehart and Winston, 1960.

Hediger, H. *Wild Animals in Captivity*. New York: Dover, 1964.

Holmberg, A. R. *Nomads of the Long Bow*. Garden City, N.Y.: Natural History Press, 1969.

Kalish, R. A. "The effects of Death upon the Family." In L. Pearson, ed. *Death and Dying.* Cleveland: Case Western Reserve University Press, 1969.

Kastenbaum, R. The Interpersonal Context of Death in a Geriatric Institution. Paper presented at annual meeting of the Gerontological Society, Minneapolis, 1964.

Koty, J. *Die Behandlung der Alten und Kranken bei den Naturvolkern.* Stuttgart: W. Kohlhammer, 1933.

Lee, R. B. "Kung Bushmen Subsistence: An Input–Output Analysis." In A. P. Vayda, ed. *Environment and Cultural Behavior.* Garden City, N.Y.: Natural History Press, 1969.

———, and I. De Vore. *Man the Hunter.* Chicago: Aldine, 1968.

Lieberman, M. "The Relationship of Mortality Rates to Entrance to a Home for the Aged." *Geriatrics,* 16 (1961), 515–519.

Linton, R. "Age and Sex Categories." *American Sociological Review* 7 (1942), 589–603.

Maxwell, R. J. "Onstage and Offstage Sex: Exploring an Hypothesis." *Cornell Journal of Social Relations,* 1 (1967), 75–84.

———. "The Changing Status of Elders in a Polynesian Society. *Aging and Human Development,* 1 (1970), 137–146.

Maxwell, R. J., and P. Silverman. "An Informational Approach to the Treatment of the Aged: Responses to Old People in Siberia and Ireland." Paper read at the Gerontological Society, Houston. October 1971.

Mead, M. *New Lives for Old: Cultural Transformation—Manus 1928–1953.* New York: Morrow, 1956.

Menzel, H. "A New Coefficient for Scalogram Analysis." *Public Opinion Quarterly,* 17 (1953), 268–280.

Murdock, G. P. "World Sampling Provinces." *Ethnology,* 7 (1968), 305–326.

Nash, M. *Primitive and Peasant Economic Systems.* San Francisco: Chandler, 1966.

Okada, Y. "Changing Family Relationships of Older People in Japan During the Last Fifty Years." In C. Tibbitts and W. Donahue, eds. *Social and Psychological Aspects of Aging.* New York: Columbia University Press, 1962a.

———. "The Aged in Rural and Urban Japan." In C. Tibbitts and W. Donahue, eds. *Social and Psychological Aspects of Aging.* New York: Columbia University Press, 1962b.

Olson, R. L. *Chumash Prehistory. University of California Publications in American Archaeology and Ethnology,* 28 (1930), 1–21.

Riley, M. W., and A. Foner. *Aging and Society: An Inventory of Research Findings,* vol. 1. New York: Russell Sage Foundation, 1968.

Roberts, J. M. *Three Navaho Households: A Comparative Study in Small Group Culture. Peabody Mus. Harvard Univ. Papers* 40, 3, 1951.

———. *Zuni Daily Life.* University of Nebraska Laboratory of Anthropology, Notebook 3, Monograph 2, 1956.

———. "Zuni." In F. R. Kluckhohn and F. L. Strodtbeck, eds. *Variations in Value Orientations.* New York: Harper & Row, 1961.

———. "The Self-Management of Cultures." In W. Goodenough, ed. *Explorations in Cultural Anthropology.* New York: McGraw-Hill, 1964.

———, and B. Sutton-Smith. "Child Training and Game Involvement." *Ethnology,* 1 (1962), 166–185.

Rowe, W. L. "The Middle and Later Years in Indian Society." In R. W. Kleemeier, ed. *Aging and Leisure.* New York: Oxford University Press, 1961.

Sahlins, M. D., and E. R. Service. *Evolution and Culture.* Ann Arbor: University of Michigan Press, 1960.

Shelton, A. J. Igbo Child-rearing, Eldership, and Dependence: A Comparison. In R. A. Kalish, ed. *The Dependencies of Old People.* Institute of Gerontology Occasional Papers, no. 6, University of Michigan–Wayne State University, 1969.

Silverman, P. "Local Elites and the Image of a Nation: The Incorporation of Barotseland Within Zambia." Unpublished doctoral dissertation, Cornell University, Ithaca, N.Y., 1968.

———, and R. J. Maxwell. "Models of Aging: China and Western Tibet." Paper read at the meetings of the American Anthropological Association, New York City, November 1971.

———, and ———. "An Anthropological Approach to the Study of the Aged." Paper read at the meetings of the Gerontological Society, San Juan, Puerto Rico, December 1972.

———, and ———. "A Comparative Study of Categories of Deference Displays Towards Old People." Paper read at the meetings of the Gerontological Society, Louisville, Kentucky, October 1975.

Simmons, L. W. *The Role of the Aged in Primitive Society.* New Haven: Yale University Press, 1945.

Spencer, P. *The Samburu: A Study of Gerontocracy in a Nomadic Tribe.* Berkeley: University of California Press, 1965.

Valentine, C. A. *Masks and Men in a Melanesian Society.* Lawrence: University of Kansas Press, 1962.

White, L. A. *The Science of Culture.* New York: Grove Press, 1949.

———. *The Evolution of Culture.* New York: McGraw-Hill, 1959.

Whiting, J. W. M. "Effects of Climate on Certain Cultural Practices." In W. Goodenough, ed. *Explorations in Cultural Anthropology.* New York: McGraw-Hill, 1964.

———. "Methods and Problems in Cross-Cultural Research." In G. Lindzey and E. Aronson, eds. *The Handbook of Social Psychology,* vol. 2, 2d ed. Reading, Mass.: Addison–Wesley, 1968.

Young, F. W. *Initiation Ceremonies: A Cross-Cultural Study of Status Dramatization.* New York: Bobbs–Merrill, 1965.

THE CHANGING STATUS OF ELDERS IN A POLYNESIAN SOCIETY | 3

The research described in the previous chapter has shown that the status of the aged varies from society to society. A few examples will help to recapitulate. Like many nomadic hunters and gatherers, the Siriono of the Bolivian highlands abandoned their aged and infirm without ceremony (Holmberg 1969). Similarly, certain inland Eskimo groups abandoned their old and sick, although this practice may have been less widespread among the Eskimo than believed (Hughes 1961).

The Chinese, on the other hand, venerated their aged, who were after all but one step removed from the guardians of the hearth, the ancestors. The *Li Chi*, or Book of Ritual, one of the classics of Chinese literature which political and social aspirants were required to learn, deals mostly with the care of the aged. Indeed, respect for the aged was so deeply ingrained in the Chinese that Gray (1878: 239) describes a law which, in the case of parricide, "expressly declares that not only shall the offender be subjected to a lingering death, but that the schoolmaster who instructed him in his youth shall be decapitated, and that the bones of his grandfathers shall be exhumed and scattered to the winds."

Simmons's volume (1945) suggests some of the determinants of the treatment of the aged. Case studies abound on how the aged fare (for example, Arth 1965; Holmberg 1961; Shelton 1965; Smith 1961; Spencer 1965; and see especially Holmes 1972).

These studies, however valuable, are essentially synchronic. They have directed much attention to the status of the aged but relatively little to changes in that status as a result of contact with Western culture. The intent here is to illustrate some of these changes as they occurred and are occurring now in Samoa, an island society in western Polynesia. The suggestion here is that the traditional authority of the elders has been undermined by a relatively recent influx of Western cultural and economic traits, particularly the introduction of a market exchange system.

Samoan Social Structure

The Samoan islands are found in the south Pacific about midway between Hawaii and Australia and cover somewhat more than 1,200 square miles, an area a bit larger than Rhode Island. The six major islands are formed by volcanic peaks creating a mountainous and rugged setting. They were settled by canoeloads of voyagers from the west, perhaps as early as 1,000 B.C. From Samoa, most probably, the other Polynesian islands were settled. The Samoans today are racially mixed—tall, brown-skinned, robust.

Samoan subsistence originally depended on gathering wild plant foods such as the coconut, cultivating roots and tubers, raising pigs and chickens, and catching fish and other sea creatures. The economy was in no sense specialized, although there was a division of labor between the sexes and between age groups, and, by the time of Western contact in the eighteenth century, such craftsmen as carpenters were beginning to emerge. Aside from occasional typhoons, which caused temporary shortages, the population was subject to no natural catastrophes and there was food enough for all.

The kinship unit was the extended family, a group of relatives from both the male and female sides. Generally, they resided in a group of thatch-roofed huts along with other extended families in a single village. The village, then, consisted of several extended families living side by side, each of them headed by an elected chief. There were few absolute requirements for chieftainship, but ordinarily families were led by elderly men, rarely women, who were loyal to their kinsmen and socially skilled. The person who was elected to the chieftainship dropped his personal name and was addressed by title instead. Titles varied considerably within the village in the degree of prestige accorded their holders. The more socially competent and economically successful chiefs acquired great political influence as representatives of their families at the village council.

A chief was normally succeeded by his oldest son, but arrangements for succession were flexible. The concern of paramount importance was the welfare of the family; and if the oldest son was not deemed qualified, someone else was chosen. The prestige of a chief was expressed through the deference behavior of other villagers. For example, at family gatherings he was the first to be served kava, a spicy, mildly psychotropic beverage of ceremonial significance; he was the first served at feasts and was awarded the choicest parts of the pig. People of lesser status were obliged to sit when he entered a room and to crouch and mutter apologies if they needed to walk past him or around him. Finally, if others addressed him, they used a ritualized, highly formal language with a rather different lexicon in order to indicate their respect, though it was impolite for a chief to use this ceremonial language when speaking about himself. If a chief was not shown proper respect, the slight was considered an insult by his entire family.

In return for all this, a chief had dual responsibilities, as a member of the family on the one hand, and as a member of the village on the other. First, within the family itself he acted as leader in the consideration of important family matters. He administered the land owned corporately by the extended family, deciding who should work which plots; he arbitrated family disputes; when necessary, he appropriated lesser chiefs' titles and assigned them to family members. In general, a chief saw to it that there was as much harmony and as little friction as possible among those who had elected him head of the family.

As a member of the village, he represented his family at the periodic meetings of the council of chiefs; he assumed his proper role in such cooperative community affairs as fishing, warfare, and the construction of community-owned buildings; and, depending on his prestige, he arbitrated disputes between families and sometimes between villages. A chief had to play his role with deliberation (whether feigned or real), dignity, and a suitable display of pomp.

The political and moral power of a chief was reinforced by his control over the exchange of valued material goods. His control differed according to whether the exchange of goods was taking place within his own family or between his family and another.

His extended family was of course made up of several conjugal units, each consisting of a man, his wife, their children, and perhaps other resident kinsmen. These conjugal units were largely in charge of their own subsistence affairs. They worked the land assigned to them, often fished and hunted by themselves, and raised their own domestic animals. Whenever anything suggestive of a food surplus resulted from their labors—a fishing expedition, a crop harvest, or the killing of a pig—the conjugal unit was obliged to send a large portion of the surplus to the chief as an outright gift. The chief then set aside part of this for the use of his own wife and children, divided the rest into smaller portions, and sent these around to the other members of his extended family. Thus he acted as a guidance mechanism in the circulation of surplus food within the extended family.

In addition, chiefs took responsibility on occasions such as funerals, visits of large parties from other villages, and, after Western contact, church dedications, when enormous quantities of food and other materials were exchanged between extended families. If, for example, a villager from another family died, it was a chief's duty to see that a suitable amount of valuable goods, such as finely woven mats, bark cloth, and food, was presented to the extended family of the dead person. The chief of the deceased's family had the responsibility of preparing an elaborate feast, during which quantities of food were given to the other families in the village. In other words, each extended family, under the leadership of its chief, was responsible only for its own performance at community ceremonies, and no overall figure was in charge of the exchange.

The picture presented here is a somewhat telescoped but roughly accurate description of two models of sharing, that between and that within families. Exchange between families corresponds in some ways to what the economist Polanyi has called a reciprocal economy; exchange within families corresponds to a redistributive economy. It will be seen later how these are decaying under the impact of a recently introduced system of indirect exchange, dependent on the presence of money and markets (Polanyi 1953).

Older women in Samoa derived their status from that of their husbands. Although a chief's wife did not have the political power of her husband, she nevertheless engaged in a substantial amount of backstage manipulation, and her presence generated similar deference behavior in the villagers. When wives met for discussion, for example, they were served kava in the order that their husbands would have been served.

The exercise of this kind of power requires a certain minimum of physical vigor, and, like everyone else, chiefs grow older. A man might go on until he died in office. Or he might continue in office until he had grown so feeble that his authority was informally passed on to another family elder or to his oldest son. Grattan (1948: 15) describes another option open to an aging chief.

Near the end of a long life of service for the family, a matai [chief] may feel the burden of his position pressing too heavily upon his aged shoulders. He may then call his family together and after expressing his wish to retire from the burden of leadership, he may ask the family to choose some other holder of the title. . . . Thereafter, custom will permit him to take his usual place in the assembly of chiefs and orators without being troubled . . . as regards the family or the village. His cup will be distributed to him as usual in kava ceremonies. . . . Such a retired matai will wisely leave the greater part of the duties to his successor, putting forward an opinion occasionally without ostentation to help the new matai, who, if he wishes to win the approbation both of his predecessor and the village, will be careful from time to time to show respect and recognition to the old man. And so the latter ends his days in peace and quietness, treated with that peculiar delicacy and consideration of which Samoan custom can be so pleasantly capable when the circumstances are favorable.

The infirm aged are cared for with matter-of-fact kindness within the family, mostly by women and older children. The unexpected death of a person in full vigor disrupts the social fabric, but death among the aged is accepted with some equanimity. The prevailing attitude in the aged is expressed in one elder's comment: "Why worry? When my time comes, I'll just lay down and go." This fatalistic attitude toward illness and death has been noticed by other observers (Churchill 1920).

Distinctions existed between titled and untitled men, and not every aged man was a chief. But elderly untitled men were very much respected by the young, in part because of their accumulated wealth, their intrafamilial influence, and their wisdom and experience, and in part simply because they had survived into old age, which few accomplished in the absence of modern medical care. In any case, despite distinctions, the desire to be a chief was universal, and with a record of continuing useful family service, a man's chances of being elected were good, so that the following statements, though dealing primarily with chiefs, may be taken as paradigmatic of the status of aged males in Samoa.

Contact with the West

The Samoan Islands were discovered by the Dutch captain Jacob Roggeveen in 1722, but aside from occasional visits by Western ships, the islanders had little contact with Europeans or Americans until missionaries arrived in 1830. This was rather late in Polynesia, for by that time Hawaii had already undergone a great deal of culture change, and Tahiti, Tonga, and New Zealand had already been missionized. To some extent the delay may have stemmed from the fierce reputation that Samoans had acquired from the accounts of early explorers.

In 1830 the ubiquitous preacher John Williams landed in Samoa. With the cooperation of a powerful and accommodating chief, he and his colleagues rapidly converted the Samoans to Christianity. As the Samoans had never been particularly religious their social organization was little changed after conversion. Following the missionary enterprises, a succession of American whalers, British colonials, and German traders arrived. In 1900 the islands were divided, with western Samoa going to Germany, eastern Samoa to the United States. In 1914 New Zealand took control of the western part and in 1962 it became the first country in Oceania to achieve independence. American Samoa, where Maxwell spent twenty-two months conducting research in 1965 and 1966, concerns us here.

American Samoa had been ruled with relative benevolence by the U.S. Navy. Infrequent American ships used Pago Pago, with its fine harbor, as a coaling station and the small number of naval personnel were accepted by the Samoans. Officers, with their elaborate ceremonial costumes, rituals, symbols of office, and so on, were understood to be chiefs, while the enlisted men were understood to be untitled. The navy treated the chiefs with dignity, maintained dispensaries around the islands, and kept relationships amicable. World War II saw a vast increase in the number of military personnel in the islands; more Western goods were introduced; and the Americans so often violated certain native belief systems that they were brought under closer scrutiny by local leaders. Everyone knew, for example, that ghosts were likely to attack and injure anyone walking alone through the jungle after dark, yet marines stood solitary watch, unharmed, among the palm trees at night. Was it possible that ghosts were not as powerful as had been thought?

This influx of Western traits had little impact on the structure of

Samoan society itself, largely because the economic base remained the same. Authority still lay with the chiefs, who expected and received gifts of food and goods and who supervised the exchange of goods between families. The younger men provided the manpower, the older men supplied the guidance. After the war, the troops departed and the Samoans settled into a life-style more or less like their prewar existence. Unknown to the majority of the populace, however, the war years had created a framework for rapid sociocultural change.

During the postwar period certain critical trends became apparent. First, transportation facilities were expanded rapidly. Roads around the largest island of Tutuila were being improved, giving people in outlying villages easy access to Pago Pago, where most of the Americans and part-Samoans lived, and where wage-work was available and life had a decidedly Western flavor.

Second, the population was becoming literate. Some had learned a little English in school; others had picked up the language from the troops. Many Samoans were now able to read the news bulletins and small newspapers which had been printed for years. The influence of reading matter on a culture that has previously passed on information through oral tradition cannot be overestimated. Written archives could now gradually replace older men and women who served the community as data banks. And, as if to facilitate the process of replacing the elderly, Western Samoa established its first radio broadcasting station in 1948, and American Samoa followed suit in 1952. Programs were as much concerned with instruction in tasks like horticulture as they were with entertainment—a further incursion into the pool of data controlled by the older and more experienced members of the community (Keesing and Keesing 1956: 156–182; Roberts 1964).

Finally, material items of Western culture came to have a great impact on Samoan life. Those items dealing merely with the storage of food were of enormous importance. Foodsharing customs can be partly explained in ecological terms, the climate of Samoa being such that food spoiled quickly unless consumed. (The only significant food especially prepared for storage was a kind of tough biscuit of fermented breadfruit, typically made following a typhoon, when many breadfruit trees had been knocked down.) The food given to others, however, was not forever gone. Sooner or later, others would have a surplus and would return a like amount. The effect was that neighbors acted as storage bins for food.

The family chiefs were the most important figures in the circulation of food within the village, and they extracted a share for the consumption of their own conjugal families. But with the increasing postwar exposure to varieties of canned and dried foods, there was less incentive to share food with others. And with the introduction of the refrigerator, following electrification of the more remote communities, food exchange was further slowed. As a result, not only was the chief given fewer outright gifts of food, but he was denied the share he would have received had food exchange continued at its prewar pace.

The naval administration of American Samoa was dissolved in 1951 and the territory transferred to the U.S. Department of the Interior. The new administration changed little in the formal political organization of Samoan society. Under the governor of American Samoa, the chiefs held as much political and legal power as before. To be sure, the governor was empowered to overrule any law the chiefs might enact, and to ignore any suggestions they might make, but he generally exercised more subtle means of control.

In 1964, however, the government revamped the entire educational system, consolidating the schools at every level, eliminating many poorly run elementary schools in outlying districts, and introducing a highly structured system of educational television. At about the same time, a multimillion dollar hotel was constructed in the vicinity of Pago Pago, providing wage-work for hundreds of young Samoan men and women. The hotel is now staffed entirely by Samoans and part-Samoans, except for the manager. A recently constructed modern airport opened new opportunities for work as well.

In 1962 there were 5,833 Samoans and part-Samoans engaged in wage-work, the majority of them government employees. This number constitutes 42 percent of the available labor force, male and female (*American Samoa Governor's Report* 1962). And since the construction of the hotel, the airport, and consolidated schools, the number of Samoans with wage-work experience has gone up considerably. This is undoubtedly a secular or long-term trend. Wage-work and the regular biweekly pay check have become indispensable parts of most households today.

All other sources of subsistence seem to be declining in importance despite financial rewards for the adults who systematically work their family gardens, called plantations. At the open marketplace in Pago Pago, for example, one may buy local produce—taro, yams, bananas, pineapples—at relatively high prices. Pineapples that might cost 49 cents in an American supermarket cost 75 cents in the marketplace. The demand is greater than the supply, so that some of this produce must be imported from Western Samoa and elsewhere. However, the plantations are not used to their capacity because Western foods are becoming more important and because more of the young adults are staying in school, working locally for wages, or migrating elsewhere, thus becoming unavailable as labor for the land.

Furthermore, there seems to be a selective recruitment of wage-workers from among the younger and more ambitious people. Most wage-work in Samoa consists of manual labor—construction, maintenance, road work—under a blazing tropical sun, six days a week, for a starting wage of about 45 cents an hour. These jobs are not for the elderly, the weak, or the lazy. Samoans at home, working their plantations pretty much when they felt like it, could still provide food for their families. Some do exactly this, but they are mostly the elderly or the less Westernized young adults.

Similarly, many of the more talented young men and women are completing high school and entering institutions of higher learning, either in the local teacher training schools or in colleges and universities in the United States. By 1966, for example, the government of American Samoa had sent 110 students abroad on scholarships, in addition to those students being supported by their families (reported in the *Samoan Times*, April 4, 1966). And greater numbers of working young people are emigrating to America simply because wages are higher there and the life-style seems appealing.

Those who live abroad send some part of their pay to their parents and to their family chiefs, just as they would have shared their fishing catches. Whether distant sons support their families with the same enthusiasm as they would if they were still living at home cannot be determined. But in any case, since this transfer of wealth is not part of face-to-face interaction, the sender need not feel embarrassed if the gift is smaller than it might be. Furthermore, the chief has no way of knowing exactly how bountiful an emigrant's catch was.

Discussion

The impingement of Western culture on life in American Samoa has become pronounced since World War II and especially since 1951 when its administration became a duty of the U.S. Department of the Interior. Westernization has become apparent through the expansion of facilities for transportation, communication, and education, all of which have exposed young Samoans to American concepts of autonomy and private property, and which have rendered the elderly less and less useful as information sources. The influence of American culture on Samoan life is also evident in the introduction of items that facilitate food storage, as well as in the increasing dependence of the Samoan family and the economy in general upon wages, earned primarily by the young.

What effect does this have on the status of the elders in Samoa? Two examples are offered to reinforce the impact of these continuing changes. The first is taken directly from an interview recorded in the field. The informant is a man in his mid-twenties, a graduate of a small college in the United States, currently a teacher in one of the consolidated high schools. His statements are fairly typical for a young man of his background.

Q: Would like to have a title?
A: Title? Oh, you mean a chief title? No. I sure would like to get rid of this chief system.
Q: Why?
A: It seems to me that the chiefs of the clans are taking advantage of the people who don't hold titles. Nowadays some of the young people are getting used to some of the Western ideas. It used to be that everybody in the family would work and give their whole pay check to the chief, and he would distribute the money to the members of the family. But I would like to work and give the money away the way I want. I would not give it to the chief to distribute. Maybe fifty years ago, if somebody went fishing, he would come back and give all the fish to the chief. And the chief would distribute them. But now, if I want to go fishing, I don't give any to the chief. If I want to eat them all, I eat them all. My family has asked me several times to try to get a title, and I say: "No—my name is Va'afatu Tupiano, and I'll die being Va'afatu Tupiano!" Sometimes the chief doesn't know anything. Sometimes people want to change things and the Samoans say, "Let's not. It's tradition." But I think if it's for the good of the people, a change should be made. I'm not afraid of change. The old people do not like their children to go to American dances. I don't know anything about American dancing, but I say if they want to go, let them go.

Another informant, a man of 36 who worked in the Pago Pago area, was approached in the interviewer's presence by an older kinsman. The younger man, Peter, asked the old man, Ulu, to sit down. Ulu did so. He was a chief, albeit a minor chief, and he curled his legs under him on the floor mat, smoothed the folds of his loincloth, and bending his cropped and grizzled head, spoke slowly and with dignified deliberation about the responsibilities of chieftainship. Peter nodded his head and listened earnestly, waiting for the old man to finish. Ulu finally put it to Peter that there was a vacancy in one of the titles of the family and, since he knew Peter to be industrious and loyal, he would very much like Peter to think about assuming the title and becoming a chief himself.

Peter politely thanked Ulu for being so generous in his judgments, but pointed out that he had spent several years in the Coast Guard and several years afterwards working in Honolulu. These experiences, Peter said, had given him too many new ideas to perform well as a chief. He pointed out that other men in the family who were older and more tradition-oriented would be more suitable to become head of the family.

When Ulu had gone, Peter turned to the interviewer and grimaced. "I don't want none of that chief stuff! Who cares about chief any more?" He went on to say that in his village—where there were about eighteen chiefs—only one family shared its food with the chief the way they did in the old days. The other families still tendered gifts of food and goods to their chiefs, but not the way they used to. The chief had all sorts of responsibilities; he had to worry all the time, he couldn't get drunk at parties, and he received too little in return.

Peter was talking about the irrelevance of the elders, and about the discrepancy in the allocation of economic power, which accrued more and more to the young, and political power, which still rested formally in the hands of the elderly. Family heads, who previously commanded the distribution of wealth, now find themselves with a decreasing economic basis for their political authority. And they themselves are not unaware that their power is being threatened from many sides. One of their reasons for opposing the government-sponsored house-building program following the typhoon of 1966 was fear that they would lose their authority over the administration of the land (editorial, *Samoan Times*, May 9, 1966).

The moral influence of chiefs is waning even within their own families, as youngsters move out from under their scrutiny and control and establish themselves as wage earners elsewhere. An added difficulty is that these restless young men are precisely the ones who would once have been bold and daring warriors, owing allegiance to no controlling agent higher than the head of the family. Lost in the anonymity of an urban setting, they cause a disproportionate amount of trouble. A Honolulu newspaper recently conducted a survey of forty-three Samoan households in Hawaii in an attempt to discover some of the reasons for this. The results should prove interesting.

Summary

The situation described in American Samoa is not unique. The more young wage earners control the flow of wealth, the more incentive there is for other young people to enter wage-work themselves. These generalizations have been phrased in qualitative terms, but there is empirical evidence elsewhere (Ember 1964) that the introduction of money and wage-work into the economy of Samoan villages is associated with the decay of the traditional power structure. There are further studies suggesting that the processes outlined here are not restricted to Polynesia; they occur among such widely different people as the urban Chinese (Yap 1962), the relatively isolated Havasupai of Arizona (Smithson 1959: 130), and the cattleherding Hottentot of South Africa (Schultze 1907: 102).

Nothing here is meant to imply that Samoan elders, chiefs or otherwise, are treated with contempt. Indeed, the opposite is true. Younger persons, whatever work they are engaged in and wherever they are located, unfailingly contribute money and other gifts to the family through the chief, and they invariably show respect for elders in direct encounters. Yet it is evident that recent developments in a situation of culture contact have undermined the traditional authority of elders in Samoa making them less functional as controllers of information and wealth. With the ongoing Americanization of the islands and their peoples, this trend can be expected to continue.

References

American Samoa Governor's Report to the Secretary of the Interior. Washington, D.C. Government Printing Office, 1962.

Arth, M. J. "The Role of the Aged in a West African Village." *Gerontologist*, 5, part 2 (1965), 43.

Churchill, L. P. *Samoa 'Uma.* London: Sampson, Low, Marsten, 1920.

Ember, M. "Commercialization and Political Change in American Samoa." In W. Goodenough, ed. *Explorations in Cultural Anthropology.* New York: McGraw-Hill, 1964.

Grattan, F. J. H. *An Introduction to Samoan Custom.* Apia: Samoa Printing and Publishing Co., 1948.

Gray, J. H. *China: A History of the Laws, Manners, and Customs of the People I.* London: Macmillan, 1878.

Holmberg, A. R. "Age in the Andes." In R. W. Kleemeier, ed. *Aging and Leisure.* New York: Oxford University Press, 1961.

————. *Nomads of the Long Bow.* Garden City, N.Y.: Natural History Press, 1969.

Holmes, L. D. "The Role and Status of the Aged in a Changing Samoa." In D. O. Cowgill and L. D. Holmes, eds. *Aging and Modernization.* N.Y.: Appleton–Century–Crofts, 1972.

Hughes, C. C. "The Concept and Use of Time in the Middle Years: The St. Lawrence Island Eskimo." In R. W. Kleemeier, ed. *Aging and Leisure.* New York: Oxford University Press, 1961.

Keesing, F. M., and M. M. Keesing. *Elite Communication in Samoa: A Study of Leadership.* Stanford, Calif.: Stanford University Press, 1956.

Li Chi (The Book of Ritual). Translated by James Legge. Sacred Books of the East. Oxford: Oxford University Press, 1879–1885.

Polanyi, K. *Semantics of General Economic History,* rev. ed. New York: Columbia University Research, Project on "Origins of Economic Institutions," 1953.

Roberts, J. M. "The Self-Management of Cultures." In W. Goodenough, ed. *Explorations in Cultural Anthropology.* New York: McGraw-Hill, 1964.

Schultze, L. *Aus Namaland und Kalahari.* Jena. Translated and incorporated into the Human Relations Area Files, 1907.

Shelton, A. J. "Ibo Aging and Eldership: Notes for Gerontologists and Others." *Gerontologist,* 5 (1965), 20–23.

Simmons, L. W. *The Role of the Aged in Primitive Society.* New Haven: Yale University Press, 1945.

Smith, R. J. "Cultural Differences in the Life Cycle and the Concept of Time." In R. W. Kleemeier, ed. *Aging and Leisure.* New York: Oxford University Press, 1961.

Smithson, C. "The Havasupai Woman." *Anthropological Papers.* Salt Lake City: University of Utah, 1959.

Spencer, P. *The Samburu: A Study of Gerontocracy in a Nomadic Tribe.* Berkeley: University of California Press, 1965.

Yap, P. M. "Aging in Underdeveloped Asian Countries." In C. Tibbitts and W. Donahue. *Social and Psychological Aspects of Aging: Aging Around the World.* New York: Columbia University Press, 1962.

AGING AND RACE | 4

In this chapter we turn our focus on the life of the elderly among American Indians and black Americans. We are especially concerned with the influences of institutional structures and change on their subsistence and health care. Although the elderly of other ethnic groups could have been selected, these groups have been chosen to highlight the nature of poverty and aging in America. A discussion follows of the consequences of being poor, elderly, and black or American Indian in a youth-oriented society where people of European origin predominate.

American Indian Elderly

The suffering of elderly American Indians has only recently begun to get close attention in the mass media and in scientific literature (Levy 1967: 225). In the United States, where we pay so much lip service to humanitarian ideals, many aging American Indians are compelled to struggle for biological survival and human dignity on federally controlled reservations.

Recently the number of American Indians in the U.S. population was set at 791,838 (*Facts* 1971: 4), of whom some 477,500 lived on reservations. Although many leave reservations each year, most of the migrants are youthful tribal members. For the most part, the elderly remain behind (Doherty, 1971: 17–18).

Data on reservation-based American Indians indicate that a family of three had an average yearly income of $1,500 in 1968 (Cahn 1969). This figure was half the minimum income required for subsistence according to the Bureau of Labor Statistics. Longevity statistics showed the average American Indian lifespan to be 44 years; impoverished living conditions and high infant mortality contribute heavily to this average.

CONTRASTING VALUES

Some understanding of the social nature of aging among American Indians can be gained by contrasting Euroamerican images of the elderly and beliefs about them with those held by American Indians themselves. Some useful insights are gleaned from Wax and Thomas (1961) and from a recent report by the National Council on Aging focusing on a comparison between the modes of "Indian Values as Opposed to Non-Indian Values" ("Indian Values" 1967).

American Indian Customs	*Euroamerican Customs*[1]
Age: Respect is for the elders. Experience is felt to bring knowledge. So the older one is, the more knowledgeable he is. No effort is made to conceal white hair or other signs of age.	Youth: Millions of dollars are spent yearly for hair dyes, makeup, and other items intended to make older people look younger. Whole towns have sprung up in the U.S. which advertise youthful living in communities designed for "senior citizens."
Extended family: Aunts are often considered mothers. Uncles may be called fathers, and some cousins are treated as brothers and sisers of the immediate family. Clan members are considered relatives.	Nuclear family:[2] The biological family (or conjugal pair and offspring) is of utmost importance. Relationships are limited to this group and for the most part exclude even close relatives.

In addition to the value that American Indians place on sustained interactions with relatives, the elderly are revered for their wisdom. Increasing chronological age is not associated with increasing social disability. On the contrary, growing old—and the cumulative knowledge that this implies—is associated with increasing rank.

Euroamerican practices suggest images of the elderly which are in sharp contrast. As indicated in a 1969 report of the U.S. Senate's Special Committee on Aging: "Both government and private industry seem to regard earlier and earlier retirement, or in some cases enforced unemployment, as inevitable and perhaps desirable" ("Employment Aspects," 1969: iii). Such practices as these would force the elderly out of socially useful and personally gratifying roles. Furthermore, the institutionalization of retirement codes developed by and supported in Euroamerican groups—which are then imposed on all workers—may have progressively devastating effect on the economic ability of the elderly to sustain themselves, especially those who belong to minority groups.

ECONOMIC DISADVANTAGES

In 1964, one-half of all American Indian families had incomes of less than $2,000 per year (Doherty 1971: 19; Brinker 1968: 440). In 1967 the unemployment rate for all American Indians on reservations was 37.3 percent, as compared to 2.3 percent for other Americans (Doherty 1971: 21). Specific figures on unemployment among the elderly were not given. However, based on American employment practices, it seems reasonable to hypothesize that their income and employment levels were considerably lower than the figures representing American Indians in general. That this hypothesis is reasonable is suggested by the kinds of wage-work opened to them in recent years. Many of the jobs, such as construction and assembly-line work, are compatible with the physical strength of the young rather than the elderly (Doherty 1971: 21–22; *Self-Determination* 1971: 30–43).

INADEQUACY OF HEALTH CARE

In addition to their financial impoverishment, the elderly on Indian reservations are faced with a critical shortage of hospital and clinic facilities. It is commonplace for the aged on reservations to travel close to a hundred miles to a hospital clinic, only to find two or three hundred people in line ahead of them (Cahn 1969: 66). Large numbers of the elderly are forced to leave hospitals and clinics untreated. "The U.S. Public Health Service estimates that in 1966 only one-third of the total beneficiary population received dental examinations, and that less than a fourth of those who needed treatment received it" (Cahn 1969: 60).

To make matters worse, in 1968 Congress cut by one-sixth the allocation of manpower and other resources to the Public Health Service (PHS). Included among those cut back were nurses and supportive staff. Partly as a result of the cutbacks, the PHS has adopted a crisis-oriented treatment program which focuses medical care on "temporary cures rather than attacking underlying environmental and nutritional causes" of illness (Cahn 1969: 60–62).

It is clear from the foregoing sketch that a youth-oriented Euroamerican culture, a devaluation of older workers, and a crisis-oriented health service have converged to form an oppressive social structure that has aging American Indians caught in its grip. On federally administered reservations, theirs is an existence of extreme poverty, alienation from traditional styles of life, and relative powerlessness to change their conditions.

African American Elderly

Aged African Americans have also known a history of social oppression and cultural alienation. However, extended family structures and strong kinship ties have contributed a degree of strength which has enabled many of the African American elderly, especially women, to carry on socially constructive lives despite an oppressive situation. A recent study reported that elderly black women—in contrast to Euroamerican men and women and black men—registered higher morale when sharing a household with someone else than when alone (Rubenstein 1971: 34–35).

The differences between aging African American men and women may be accounted for by sex-related cultural roles; these include the degrading effects of oppression on black male self-images and risk-taking behavior in contrast to the incentives given black women to play their major and continuing roles in the family and in the labor force. Low self-image and a preference for avoiding risks may be found in those who aim to curtail sustained interactions with others. In addition to the negative effects of social oppression on the family behavior of men, African American families have suffered extreme poverty.

FINANCIAL INEQUITIES

Measured against the $3,000 minimum annual income for an elderly couple and the $1,800 set as a minimum for an individual by the U.S. Bureau of Labor Statistics (BLS) in 1970, a nationwide sample revealed considerably more poverty among African American than among Euroamerican elderly in rural areas (Rubenstein 1971: 14–17). Among rural African American elderly 90.7 percent male and 96.7 percent female heads of households reported family incomes at or below the recommended minimum compared with 67.9 percent for rural Euroamerican males and 82.0 percent for females.

While the incidence of poverty was greater among rural African American elderly than it was among their urban counterparts, opposite results were reported for Euroamerican elderly. A total of 73.3 percent of urban African American males and 84.8 percent of female heads of households reported combined family incomes below the BLS minimum. Of the urban Euroamerican males and female heads of households 71.7 and 85.2 percent, respectively, reported incomes at or below the BLS standard.

In a study prepared for the National Urban League, based on 1969 census data, 33 percent of Euroamericans between the ages of 60 and 64 reported incomes below the BLS minimum for individuals. More striking was the report that 50 percent of single African Americans over 65 years of age had incomes below the recommended minimum, compared with 23 percent of Euroamericans (Lindsay 1971, table 3).

Small wonder that the African American elderly are referred to as "multiply jeopardized" (Jackson 1971: 4; Lindsay 1971). Not only are they subject to the personal degradations occasioned by institutionalized racism and by being old in a youth-oriented society, but the great majority haven't enough money to compete for goods and services (including health care) in the American marketplace.

> The older Negro man or woman who lives alone faces a daily existence even more bleak than that of married couples. $1,800 is the figure set by the BLS for a minimum sustenance budget for the lone elderly person, a budget which does not cover such basic items as medical care, carfare to the clinic, and replacement of worn out clothing [*Double Jeopardy* 1964: 6–7].

Poverty in old age is, for many African Americans, merely another phase in a lifetime of poverty. As elsewhere observed, "many elderly blacks merely retire from general public assistance to old age assistance at age 65" (Davis 1971). Thus poverty is not something peculiar to the late years of their lives.

MEDICAL DEFICIENCIES

Inadequate health care has been a major factor preventing many African Americans from sustained participation in remunerative work. While hospital and clinic facilities are theoretically available, many elderly blacks cannot afford modern medical care. In 1969, 38 percent of black males (compared with 28 percent of white males) between ages 55 and 64 were unable to work because of illness. During the same year, the ratio of African Americans to Euroamericans over 65 who were not in the labor force because of illness or physical disability was 19/9 (Davis 1971: 47–48).

Further complicating the quest for medical care is the shortage of African American medical doctors. In 1964 the National Urban League reported:

> There are only 27 Negro physicians for every 100,000 Negro persons, but there are 157 white physicians for every 100,000 white persons. . . . It is not suggested that there should be more Negro physicians because it is more desirable for Negroes to be treated by physicians of their own race; it is suggested that racial discrimination rears its ugly head in matters of health, just as it has in all other areas of Negro life [*Double Jeopardy* 1964: 15–16].

When infirm and elderly African Americans or their families go in search of nursing homes for long-term care, they can expect other problems. In several states, because there are no other places for them to go, many of the chronically ill African American elderly have been condemned to live out their lives in custodial care mental hospitals (*Double Jeopardy* 1964; Davis 1971: 48).

The absence of physicians and accessible medical service facilities is reflected in the average number of African American visits to physicians each year. According to estimates from 1970 census returns, African Americans over 65 years of age visited physicians about 4.5 times per year, as against 6.9 times for Euroamericans.[3] Given these conditions and the infant mortality differential, it is no wonder that the life expectancy of African Americans is 64.6 years, compared with 71.3 years for Euroamericans (Davis 1971: 47). Of all deaths of African Americans 65 years of age and over, 15 percent result from tuberculosis, with another 8 percent accounted for by influenza and pneumonia (*Double Jeopardy* 1964: 14). The foregoing indicates the need for a drastic overhaul in the organization of financial structures and medical services for all.

Summary

Among the 21 or more million elderly Americans, the American Indian and black groups stand out from Euroamericans as extremely poverty-stricken and in large measure deprived of life-sustaining health services. For the most part, the elderly from either minority group who are able to work have incomes that are far from sufficient to purchase the goods and health services they need. In 1970, about 75 percent of elderly American Indian families and 80 to 90 percent of elderly black families had incomes below the $3,000 minimum set by the BLS.

While health insurance coverage is a common fringe benefit for employees, most of the jobs that are open to aging Indians and blacks carry little or no health insurance (*Double Jeopardy* 1964: 17; Lindsay 1971). In addition to the discriminatory effects of low income, Indian and black elderly also lack extended care facilities and face racially discriminatory hospital practices, which, in many cases, nullify the benefits that would otherwise accrue from available cash or insurance programs.

It is clear from this study that (1) the youth-oriented values in the occupational and health care organizations of America, (2) the crisis-oriented public health service, and (3) Euroamerican discrimination against American Indians and African Americans combine to form a complex system of oppressive processes in the disservice of the elderly.

Notes

1. The term "Euroamerican customs" is used in place of "non-Indian values," which appeared as the heading for this column in the NCOA report.

2. In the NCOA report, "family" is used as a generic term to refer to both Native American and Euroamerican families. The terms "extended" and "nuclear" family are used here to help accent the differences between the two systems of values.

3. These averages are based on figures reported from two sources. The figure for African Americans is based on the mean of the means for male and female elderly, as reported in J. J. Jackson, "Some Useful Information About Black Aged," prepared for the National Caucus on the Black Aged, Center for the Study of Aging and Human Development (Durham, N.C.: Duke University Medical Center, 1971), p. 10. The figures for Euroamerican elderly are based on *Double Jeopardy* (New York: National Urban League, 1964), p. 15.

References

Brinker, Paul A. *Economic Insecurity and Social Security*. New York: Appleton–Century–Crofts, 1968.

Cahn, Edgar S., ed. *Our Brothers Keeper: The Indian in White America.* New York: World Publishing, 1969.

Davis, Donald L. "Growing Old Black." In *Employment Prospects of Aged Blacks, Chicanos, and Indians.* Washington, D.C.: National Council on the Aging, 1971.

Doherty, Edgar S., ed. "Growing Old in Indian Country." In *Employment Prospects of Aged Blacks, Chicanos, and Indians.* Washington, D.C.: National Council on the Aging, 1971.

Double Jeopardy: The Older Negro in America Today. New York: National Urban League, 1964.

"Employment Aspects of the Economics of Aging." A working paper in conjunction with the overall study. *Economics of Aging: Toward a Full Share in Abundance.* Report presented to the Special Committee on Aging, U.S. Senate, 1969.

Facts on Indian Affairs. Washington, D.C.: U.S. Department of the Interior, Bureau of Indian Affairs, 1971.

"Indian Values as Opposed to Non-Indian Values." Philadelphia: National Council on the Aging, 1967.

Jackson, Hobart C. *Advocacy for the Aged Minorities—Whose Responsibility?* Ann Arbor: University of Michigan, Institute of Gerontology, 1971.

Jackson, J. J. "Some Useful Information About Black Aged." Prepared for the National Caucus on the Black Aged, Center for the Study of Aging and Human Development. Durham, N.C.: Duke University Medical Center, 1971.

Levy, Jerold E. "The Older American Indian." In E. Grant Youmans, *Older Rural Americans.* Lexington: University of Kentucky, 1967.

Lindsay, Inabel. "Preliminary Data on Demographic Characteristics of African Americans of Middle Age and Older." Report prepared for the National Caucus of the Black Aged based on data from the U.S. Bureau of the Census and the Research Department of the National Urban League, 1971.

———. *The Multiple Hazards of Aging and Race.* Washington, D.C.: Government Printing Office, 1971.

Rubenstein, Daniel I. "An Examination of Social Participation Found Among a National Sample of Black and White Elderly." Paper presented at the annual meeting of the Eastern Psychological Association, 1971.

Self-Determination. Arizona Affiliated Tribes, Inc. Indian Community Action Project, 1971.

Wax, Rosalie H., and Robert K. Thomas. "American Indians and White People." *Phylon,* 22, 4 (Winter 1961), 305–317.

Part Two

The Disabled Elderly,
The Dying,
and Their Keepers

In the first part of this book, the studies were focused on (1) the images held of elderly persons and (2) cross-cultural variations in the treatment of the elderly as integral members of a society. This part comprises two studies of the internal organization of institutions specialized in the care of physically and mentally disabled elderly. Generally we look at the organization of these places set aside as special units to house and regulate the behavior of elderly persons no longer capable of expressing themselves, psychologically and physically, in socially acceptable ways. In addition to gaining further insights into the social significances of aging we see in the social structure of interactions between the elderly and their caretakers what might be called a *funneling effect* of increasing physical and mental disability in old age (Watson 1974). The funneling effect is suggested by the decreasing incidence of services provided by a highly trained staff, the relegation of the severely disabled to back regions of homes, and the diminution of their rights to privacy as their impairments become more severe and they come closer to death.

Elements of Institutional Structures of Aging and Dying

Whether inside or outside of specialized social settings, patterns of avoidance and restrained movement in relations with disabled persons seem more and more extreme as the disabled move farther and farther from socially approved patterns of behavior (Doob and Ecker 1970: 302-303; Le Bar 1964). For example, persons stigmatized by physically repulsive features or because they evidence bizarre mental and social behavior are often assigned places socially, ecologically, and visually segregated from areas commonly used by those who are here called the nondisabled (Foucault 1965: 42-61; Townsend 1964: 12-29).

The term *nondisabled* is used in this study to refer to persons who show in their behavior at least a minimum of socially approved abilities to care for themselves in daily activities. Walking unaided, releasing bodily excreta in socially acceptable places, and engaging in dialogue considered meaningful to others are prerequisites for recognition as a nondisabled person. By contrast, *disabled* persons are characterized by a relative absence of socially approved abilities for self-care, so that they have to depend on compensatory services provided by others.

In a study of patient groups in a hospital psychiatric ward, patterns of ecological segregation for extremely disabled patients were reported similar to patterns of segregation between the extremely disabled and nondisabled in society at large (Henry, 1964: 23-24). The youthful patients averaged 37.8 years of age, included single and married as well as male and female, and had varying personalities. The more disabled patients averaged 52.4 years of age, all were women, and all but two of them had medical diagnoses of depression.

The youthful patients frequently formed a gathering to the exclusion of the more disabled patients. In addition to differences in group memberships, the youthful group commonly gathered in a solarium where they were architecturally as well as socially segregated from the older and more disabled members in the ward unit.

These patterns of interaction between nondisabled and disabled persons suggest socially approved prohibitions against putting incompatible objects and beings together in time and place. In fact, these practices are not rare in human groups. In *The Elementary Forms of the Religious Life*, Durkheim reported that a number of societies reserved special times and places for "sacred" persons, objects, and acts from which the "profane" were excluded (Durkheim 1915: 337-347). Conversely, the profane were commonly allocated relatively exclusive places outside the sacred regions. The meanings of the labels *sacred* and *profane* are socially determined and symbolized in the conduct of members of one group seeking release or expressing institutional constraints against the presence of, or contact with members of, another group.

Closely related and in support of Durkheim's findings are Henry's observations:

> The labels "insider" and "outsider" correspond to two human groups identifiable by specific traits that are all of cultural significance and that all have important status implications in the outer world . . . "Unhappiness," as expressed in chronic depression, is an important stigmatum in the outer world, creating impulses in others to withdrawal and flight [Henry 1964: 24].

Even psychiatrists and nurses, persons professionally trained to serve the socially disabled, have been observed to resist interaction when encountering the extremely disabled elderly.

> Psychiatrists in the main have been reluctant to treat the aged due to personal anxieties regarding death; pessimism regarding the possibility of improvement and a greater interest in treating younger, more malleable people in a society in which the problems of youth have received greater emphasis [Stotsky 1968: 58-59].

In another study based on interviews with nurses working in the service of the elderly—*Where They Go to Die*—it was reported that nursing homes repel many nurses (Garvin and Burger 1968: 115). Nor do the presentations of repulsive behaviors end at the gates of nursing homes. Two recent studies of the social organization of geriatric nursing in a home for the elderly in the industrial northeastern United States showed that highly trained professional nurses systematically avoided interactions with extremely disabled elderly, while frequently interacting with nondisabled elderly who needed their attention least (Watson 1970; Watson 1972). Nurse avoidances of interactions with extremely disabled elderly may be seen as reflecting socially approved values which stigmatize old age and extreme disability, whereas youth and neuromuscular strengths are valued characteristics of social identity.[1] By stigma we mean a bodily sign that is believed to be a symbol of something unusual and bad about the being of the signifier (Goffman 1963: 1). America's youth-oriented culture values physical prowess, glamour, and attractiveness to the opposite sex. No wonder that age and disability have become attributes subject to stigmatization (Parsons 1964: 91-96, 102-103).

As described in this brief introduction to the social structure of relations between the disabled elderly and their keepers, attitudes among the nondisabled to disengage and remove from their presence extremely disabled individuals seem historically and cross-culturally pervasive. However, we have already shown in the first three chapters on aging as status passage that there are differences in values among human groups in the degree of veneration for the elderly and the roles that they may be expected to play. Partly as a consequence of the differing value systems related to social perceptions of old age, segregation may not be equally explicit or equally intense in all groups. The studies in part two will help to illustrate this point.

The specific foci of the studies in this section are threefold: (1) The organization of interactions between direct care staff, such as nurses' aides, and disabled persons is studied in two ethnically different homes for the elderly—one serving Jewish elderly and one serving elderly blacks. Since nurses and other paramedical staff are most commonly charged with assisting the elderly in meeting such daily needs as dressing, feeding, toileting, and walking, in each home our primary attention is on the organization of nursing behavior. (2) Comparisons are made between the social structures of the two homes with attention to similarities and differences in the organization of care for the mildly disabled and the severely disabled elderly. (3) Finally, the implications of these studies are considered for research and policy on the social structure of aging and dying.

Notes

1. For a theory of disengagement focused on the social behavior of the aging, and based on the assumption that "aging is an inevitable mutual withdrawal or disengagement resulting in decreased interactions between the aging person and others in the social systems he belongs to," see Elaine Cumming and William E. Henry, *Growing Old: The Process of Disengagement* (New York: Basic Books, 1961), pp. 14–16, 210–218.

References

Doob, Anthony N., and Barbara Payne Ecker. "Stigma and Compliance." *Journal of Personality and Social Psychology*, 14, 2 (1970).

Durkheim, Emile. *The Elementary Forms of the Religious Life.* New York: Free Press, 1915.

Foucault, Michel. *Madness and Civilization: A History of Insanity in the Age of Reason.* New York: New American Library, 1965.

Garvin, Richard M., and Robert E. Burger. *Where They Go to Die.* New York: Delacorte Press, 1968.

Goffman, E. *Stigma: Notes on the Management of Spoiled Identity.* Englewood Cliffs, N.J.: Prentice-Hall, 1963.

Henry, Jules. "Space and Power in a Psychiatric Unit." In Albert F. Wessen, ed. *The Psychiatric Hospital as a Social System.* Springfield, Ill.: Charles C. Thomas, 1964.

Le Bar, Frank M. "Some Implications of Ward Structure for Enculturation of Patients." In Albert F. Wessen, ed. *The Psychiatric Hospital as a Social System.* Springfield, Ill.: Charles C. Thomas, 1964.

Parsons, Talcott. *Essays in Sociological Theory.* New York: Free Press of Glencoe, 1964.

Stotsky, Bernard A. *The Elderly Patient.* New York: Grune & Stratton, 1968.

Townsend, Peter. *The Last Refuge.* London: Routledge and Kegan Paul, 1964.

Watson, Wilbur H. "Body Image and Staff-to-Resident Deportment in a Home for the Aged." *Aging and Human Development,* 1, 4 (October 1970), 345–359.

———. "Body Idiom in Social Interaction: A Field Study of Geriatric Nursing." Unpublished doctoral dissertation, Department of Sociology, University of Pennsylvania, Philadelphia, 1972.

———. "Regressive Intervention and Ethics in the Care of the Severely Impaired." *Conference Bulletin: NCSW* (November 1974).

THE INTERNAL ORDER OF A HOME FOR THE JEWISH ELDERLY | 5

Common problems seem to exist in all institutions where people routinely meet in a bounded setting. Among the most important of these is the assignment of space to the participants. Regardless of the nature of the establishment, decisions must be made about who goes where.

Although institutions for the care and treatment of the aged exist for several reasons, they function primarily because some old people are so disabled that they are hampered in maintaining themselves and moving about. The need for such institutions is undoubtedly related to the relative instability of the nuclear family in modern highly industrialized societies. Aside from their positive functions, all institutions—homes for the aged among them—have certain well-documented negative side-effects. Goffman's *Asylums* (1961) presents what is probably a prototypical case study of these effects in a psychiatric hospital.

Spatial behavior and social interaction within these institutions can be viewed as results of (1) the physical and psychological limitations of the residents, (2) protective measures taken by staff in light of these limitations and their own self-interests, and (3) the conflicts between staff and residents stimulated by differences in social and cultural attributes. In this chapter on a home for the Jewish elderly, and in the next, which is focused on a home for the black elderly, we consider each of these features of institutional structure.

The Social Structure of Space and Patterns of Interaction Between Health Professionals and Elderly Residents

Medical service offices in geriatric settings, such as nursing stations and dispensaries, can be thought of as elements in a class of places including staff lounges and staff dining rooms. Their common factor is their usefulness as places where health care personnel can take refuge from demands for service and from incessant exposure to the impositions of debilitated patients. Given this situation the following is hypothesized:

> The greater the degree of resident disability in a given behavior region of a home for the elderly, and the higher the occupational status of nursing staff, the more frequently will staff appear in medical service offices and other refuge places.

It is important here to distinguish between professional and occupational status. While registered nurses (RNs) commonly have a higher degree of technical training than licensed practical nurses (LPNs) and rank higher than LPNs in the profession of nursing, their actual occupational tasks—or work-related responsibilities—are often the same. In their responsibility for direct care, RNs and LPNs were not qualitatively different in this study. They shared responsibility for medicine passing and for planning and dispensing treatments as well as for supervising the work of aides and orderlies. It was differences in *occupational* status, or responsibility for planning, supervising, and implementing direct care performance, that were of primary interest in this study. As we shall see, however, differences in *professional* status may be more significant in distancing behavior with relation to the disabled.

The dispersion of staff for location-activities and its converse—the frequency of staff appearances at or near a nursing station—are interpreted as indicating how far, relatively, upper and lower status staff members are willing to venture into outlying subareas of a residential region and risk losing the nursing station as a shield against involvement with disabled patients (Goffman 1963: 176–177). As a specialized group of nondisabled who serve the extremely disabled elderly, nursing personnel may, to some extent, reflect the social reactions that are to be found among the nondisabled in society at large (Henry 1964: 25).

OBSERVATION SETTING

To test the hypothesis, data were collected by observing the locations of nursing staff activities over a period of six weeks, from 9 A.M. to 5 P.M., in a Jewish home for the elderly in the industrial northeastern United States. To determine the relation between patient disability and spatial behavior of nursing staff, systematic observations were made in two behavior regions, or research wards. The research wards were distinguished by directly observable and medically determined differences in the ability of patients to care for themselves and in the extent of staff intervention needed daily, such as for toileting and feeding.

Forty-four residents, five of them male and thirty-nine female, occupied the region of the extremely disabled (region A) at the time of this study. Their mean age was 84 years. The disabilities of the residents were such that most required assistance from nursing staff for such daily routines as dressing, grooming, toileting, and feeding. Furthermore, conversation between residents and staff was markedly absent. Perhaps the two most useful indicators of disability in this region were (1) the prevailing dependence on wheelchairs for movement beyond the bedrooms, ranging between 65 and 75 percent; and (2) the prevalence of anal and bladder incontinence, about 83 percent. The residents in this region were more disabled, physically and socially, than any other aggregate of residents in the home.

Seventy-two residents, ten of them male and sixty-two female, occupied the region of the nondisabled (region B). Their mean age was 83 years. In contrast to the extremely disabled, these residents were, for the most part, able to move about without wheelchairs, although some did use geriatric walkers. It was not unusual for these residents to walk the full length of the corridor and use elevators unassisted. Incontinence was rare—or rarely reported. They were generally able to dress, feed, and toilet themselves.

PROCEDURES OF OBSERVATION

Maps were drawn of the floor areas in each residential region. The map of each floor was then subdivided into rectangular areas of approximately equal size. The area of the corridor immediately in front of the nursing station—demarcated by the ends of the station counter—constituted the pivotal rectangle on each floor.

In region B, six rectangular areas were mapped out in each direction extending down the corridor from the nursing station.

Each of these subareas was demarcated by the farthest edge of the frames of each second bedroom door. A total of thirteen areas were demarcated in region B.

Region A was smaller than region B in total floor area. While the area in front of the nursing station was similarly pivotal for evenly dividing the floor area of the corridor, the rectangular subareas were limited to three in each direction. Most bedrooms in region A were four-bed dormitories, each about twice the size of a two-bed room in region B. Because the dormitory rooms were wider, the farthest edge of the frame of each bedroom door was used as the demarcation of subareas in region A.

Maps were prepared from the drawings of each floor. For reporting events observed in either region, notations were made directly on a copy of the map, showing where staff were observed and when the observations were made. Notations used for depicting staff were as follows:

RN Registered nurse
LPN Licensed practical nurse
A Nurses' aide
O Orderly
H Housekeeper (male or female)

Table 5-1 MEAN NUMBER OF NURSING STAFF PER STATUS GROUP AND TOTAL APPEARANCES OVER A SIX-WEEK PERIOD

	Mean Number of Staff per Status Group for Any Given Day During a Six-Week Period of Mapping in Each Region		*Total Number of Appearances Representing Each Status Group in Each Region Based on 48 Mappings over a Six-Week Period*	
	REGION A	REGION B	REGION A	REGION B
RNs	2	2	38	35
LPNs	6	4	108	59
A/O	8	7	128	60
H	3	3	72	36

A map of the distributions of staff for each floor was defined by the frequency distribution of notations based on forty-eight scannings of actors on the defined floor in each region.

All observations were made between the hours of 9 A.M. and 5 P.M.[1] For each of the two floors an hour-long period was randomly selected for each day, Monday through Friday, for six weeks. To avoid duplication of hours selected for sampling on any given day, mornings and afternoons were alternated as general sampling periods on each floor during the study. On any given day, one map was made for each floor. For any given time period, observations were initiated at or near the beginning of the hour.

The entrance to the corridor was the subarea where notetaking began in sampling the distribution of staff for each of the initial maps. Then, to complete a map, the observer visually scanned the floor while walking the full length of the corridor and returning to the area next to the point where the mapping began. Each day's observation began in the subarea next to the preceding day's point of origin.

When the observer entered a subarea for mapping, notations were made of each actor standing, sitting, or otherwise occupying a marked area. The observer would pause only long enough to complete his notations. If an actor appeared two or more times during the scanning period, the successive appearances were numbered. However, only the first appearance was used in plotting the frequency distributions of the location-activities of staff. When actors appeared in a doorway or on a boundary between subareas, the direction in which they faced determined the area in which their appearance was noted.

With the data collected by this procedure, frequency polygons were developed showing how often members of each status group appeared at varying distances from the nursing station in each residential region of the home.

SPATIAL BEHAVIOR OF NURSES IN RELATION TO EXTREMELY DISABLED ELDERLY

To what extent does extreme disability of residents influence the location of activities of nurses in homes for the elderly? It has been reasoned that restraint and avoidance behaviors should differ measurably between nursing staff members and between status groups when in the presence of extremely disabled elderly compared with relatively nondisabled elderly. Figure 5-1 depicts the distributions reflected in the data pertaining to the location-activity inventories of staff in the home for the aged that was the setting for this study.

As indicated by Figure 5-1, staff status group appearances in the region of the extremely disabled showed considerably higher peaks (with the exception of housekeeping) in the nursing station area

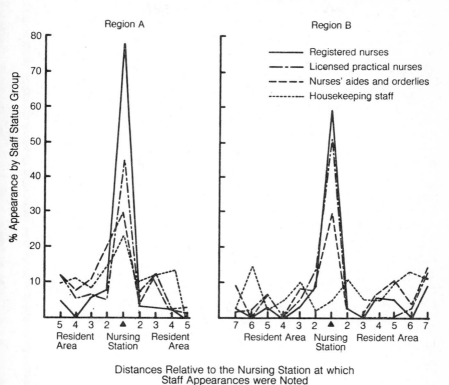

Figure 5-1 VARIATIONS IN APPEARANCES OF DIRECT CARE STAFF IN NURSING STATION AREAS IN THE REGIONS OF EXTREMELY DISABLED ELDERLY (A) AND NONDISABLED ELDERLY (B)

than their counterparts in the region of the nondisabled elderly.[2] While the distribution modes in each region are in the nursing station areas, a comparison of the graphs within floors and between floors by staff status group reveals some differences whose implications are worthy of note.

For each residential region, staff status group appearances were noted in the nursing station areas in the following rank order: (1) Registered nurses were most frequently observed in or near the nursing stations. Next were (2) licensed practical nurses, then (3) nurses' aides and orderlies, then (4) housekeepers, who appeared least in those areas. By statistical comparison, as shown in Table

5-2, RNs were observed in the nursing station of the region of the extremely disabled elderly significantly more often than they appeared in the nursing station area of the region of the nondisabled ($x^2 = 3.926$, p $<$ .05).

By contrast, LPNs made greater use of the nursing station when working in the region of the nondisabled elderly than they did when working in the region of the extremely disabled. However, for LPNs the difference between regions was not statistically significant. There were no differences in the location-activity inventories of aides/orderlies in the two regions. Finally, while the mode of housekeeping activity was irregular in the area of the nursing station in the region of the extremely disabled, the distribution of their activities in the region of the nondisabled was relatively uniform.

When RNs and LPNs were compared further, it was observed that differences between the two groups by proportion of regional appearances were all but nonexistent in the region of the nondisabled elderly. Both RNs and LPNs were observed 55 to 60 percent of the time in or near the nursing station in the region of the nondisabled.

To summarize, Figure 5-1 shows clear differences between the peaks of the modes of staff activities in the areas of the nursing stations when status groups are compared *within* regions. A comparison of staff status groups *between* regions shows observable (although not statistically significant) differences in the distribution of RN and LPN activities and in the distributions of housekeeping personnel. By contrast, the peaks of the modes for aides/orderlies are the same for the two regions—about 30 percent.

Table 5-2 PERCENTAGE OF RN APPEARANCES IN PRIMARILY RESIDENTIAL AREAS WHEN RESIDENTS ARE EXTREMELY DISABLED (REGION A) AND NONDISABLED (REGION B)

| | *Severity of Resident Impairment* | |
	EXTREMELY DISABLED	NONDISABLED
Medical service area	76	54
Primarily residential area	24	46
N	38	35

$x^2 = 3.926$, p $<$ .05
Q = .461, p $<$ .001

Factors Affecting the Disengagement of Nurses from Elderly Patients

As shown in the foregoing discussion, the relation between staff appearances in nursing station areas and patient disability is generally consistent with the basic hypothesis of this study. However, it is necessary to determine whether the observed relationship between patient disability and frequency of staff appearances in a backstage region, such as a nursing station, is anything more than spurious. In other words, the differences between staff behavior in the regions of the disabled and the nondisabled may be accounted for by factors other than differences in the appearances of disability and in service demands of the patients.

Administrative Demands as a Wedge Between Nurses and Patients In a recent study of nursing behavior in a psychiatric hospital, heavy administrative emphasis on clerical routines was found to be closely associated with infrequent interaction between upper status nurses and patients (Henry 1964: 25, 33). The value system of the general hospital, of which the psychiatric unit was a part, tended to deemphasize nurse–patient interaction and to penalize the nurse who spent time with patients (Henry 1964: 32–35). Since nursing stations are locations for record keeping as well as preparing and dispensing services in health care establishments, it is reasonable to expect that upper status nursing staff will be observed at nursing stations to an extent commensurate with the establishment's emphasis on clerical routines.

Where upper status staff are pressured into handling office details when patients need service, it is reasonable to expect that the delivery of medical services will increasingly fall to lower ranking staff. It is reasoned here that direct care activities such as grooming, feeding, and toileting are carried out in the service of disabled patients, whereas establishment or administrative routines such as clerical details are carried out in the service of nondisabled others which only secondarily or tacitly benefit the extremely disabled. Thus the administration that gives primary attention to office details and only secondary consideration to direct care of patients aims the health care establishment clearly at servicing the administration or nondisabled others rather than the patients. In some hospital units, upper status nurses have become so disengaged from interactions with patients that they have had to ask attendants or other lower ranking staff about patients in order to get the data necessary for writing routine reports (Henry 1964: 33).

Although this study was not focused on general systems of nursing organization in the administration of homes for the elderly, there are implications in Figure 5-1 that emphasis on official routines may affect the frequency of appearances of upper status nurses in resident bedrooms, sitting areas, and other places unspecialized as medical service offices. Figure 5-1 shows a greater dispersion across all subareas of each floor in the appearances of lower ranking staff than is manifest for RNs and LPNs. Furthermore, as Table 5-3 shows, the appearances of lower status staff in primarily residential regions were markedly different for residents who were severely impaired and for the nondisabled, in contrast to the appearances of upper status staff under the same conditions (Q = .232, p < .05).

When the distributions of staff appearances are compared over both residential and medical service subareas, and between regions of the severely impaired and the nondisabled elderly, aides/orderlies and housekeeping staff show a higher degree of homogeneity than RNs and LPNs in instances of subarea appearances between floors (see Figure 5-1). Statistical tests for between-subarea appearances and between-floor differences for aides/orderlies and housekeeping showed that the differences depicted in Figure 5-1 were not significant.

These findings lend general support to the hypothesized relation between severity of resident disability and distancing behavior of upper status nurses. But administrative demands for record keeping and supervision of lower ranking staff members are only one set of

Table 5-3 SEVERITY OF RESIDENT DISABILITY AND PERCENTAGE OF APPEARANCES OF UPPER STATUS AND LOWER STATUS STAFF IN PRIMARILY RESIDENTIAL AREAS IN THE REGIONS OF THE EXTREMELY DISABLED AND NONDISABLED ELDERLY

Behavior Regions	*Appearances by Staff Status Group*	
	AIDES AND ORDERLIES	RNS AND LPNS
Extremely disabled	69	59
Nondisabled	31	42
N	131	97

Q = .232, p < .05

factors that may help to explain the distancing behavior of direct care staff. Intensity of resident demands for service and staff quests for relief from the tension these demands generate are another set of factors that may help to determine the disproportionate density of upper status staff in the medical service areas rather than primarily residential areas of regions in which residents are severely impaired.

Establishing Staff Refuge Through Social Segregation of Residents The administrative demands on nurses are aggravated by the intrusion of patients who wander into nursing station areas to peer about. To some extent nursing personnel may behave toward patients as they do because they feel overworked and disgruntled and are trying to make their jobs easier by reducing the range for wandering of disoriented patients whose actions are unpredictable and occasionally disturbing (Henry 1964: 26-27).

Broadly conceived, if staff members limit resident movements to curb their wandering and thereby reduce the stress on nurses as they perform routine tasks, then a map showing regional appearances of nursing staff and residents should reveal patterns of nursing staff appearances in subregions relatively distinct from those occupied by residents. If staff restrictions on the range of resident movements increase as resident disability increases, the ecological segregation of patients should be more distinct in the region of the extremely disabled than in the region of the nondisabled. More precisely:

> If clustering of staff in relatively common subareas is aimed at avoiding interactions with residents, then areas of high staff density should have relatively low resident density. In terms of complementary relations, areas of high resident density in a given behavior region should be associated with relatively low staff densities—especially where upper status staff are involved.

It is expected that—either by agreement between staff and residents, or by staff rules about the proper locations for clusters of residents and for resident activities—modal distributions of residents will be manifest in areas used relatively little by upper status staff. To test this hypothesis, data were collected on resident appearances in the regions of the extremely disabled and the nondisabled, using the same procedures described in the foregoing discussion. However, only eight mappings were done in each region.

Resident appearances in the combined subareas were noted 500 times in the region of the severely disabled and 884 times in the region of the nondisabled. To find each point in the polygons of

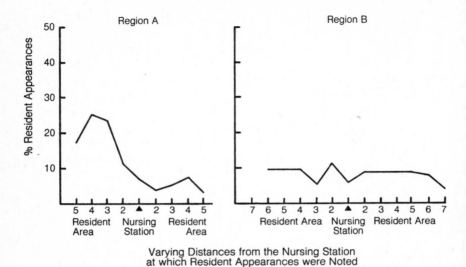

Figure 5-2 VARYING DISTANCES FROM NURSING STATION AREAS WHERE RESIDENT APPEARANCES WERE NOTED IN THE REGIONS OF EXTREMELY DISABLED (A) AND NONDISABLED (B)

Figure 5-2, the total number of resident appearances per subarea was divided by the mean number of residents living on each floor during the study. The closed ends and open ends of the corridors on each floor were demarcated by the nursing stations.

As shown in Figure 5-2, resident appearances in the region of the extremely disabled elderly were concentrated in a relatively distinct subarea. In addition, as Table 5-4 shows, the clustering of residents was in an area where resident bedrooms predominated, as contrasted with the concentration of medical service offices and related staff at the opposite end of the corridor ($x^2 = 5.29$, p $< .05$). By comparison, the region of the nondisabled elderly was characterized by relative homogeneity of resident appearances across subareas. It should be noted that, except for the nursing station, there was no concentration of medical service offices in the region of the nondisabled elderly.

When Figures 5-1 and 5-2 are compared, the curves for the distribution of upper status staff and residents intersect where the nursing stations and bedroom areas meet, with the sharpest distinctions between subareas in the region for severely disabled elderly (see

Table 5-4 PERCENTAGE DISTRIBUTIONS OF RESIDENT
APPEARANCES OVER SUBAREAS IN THE REGION OF
THE SEVERELY IMPAIRED AND IN THE REGION
OF THE NONDISABLED

Locations of Resident Appearances	Behavior Regions	
	EXTREMELY DISABLED ELDERLY	NONDISABLED ELDERLY
Resident area at closed end of corridor	75	52
Medical service and resident area at entrance to corridor	25	48
N	500	884

$$x^2 = 5.29, p < .05$$

Figure 5-3). Reasoning from the findings of a study by Pace on the
social ecology of staff-patient conduct in a psychiatric ward, the low
frequency of staff-patient events in the area indicated by the intersec-
tion of the graphs may be interpreted as an informal boundary
between subregions for patient and staff groups in the general area
of region A (Pace 1967: 581).

Insofar as distancing by nursing staff and residents is influenced
by attempts of group members to avoid violations or intrusions into
areas demarcated as territories of the other, a major impediment to
staff-patient interaction will have been established. As Sommer
observed in a study of staff-patient conduct in a mental hospital,
nurses were commonly driven back to a small area around their
station. "This is nonverbal and inexplicit, but an impressionist
painting of a mental ward would show patches of white around the
nurses' station surrounded by a sea of blue and gray representing the
patients in their drab clothing" (Sommer 1969: 81).

In Pace's study on the social organization of psychiatric aide and
patient conduct in a dayroom area—"aides were found three times as
often near the entrance to the dayroom as in the middle and rear.
They [aides] explained that it 'upset the boys back there' if they
[aides] lingered in the rear, but 'you can talk to these up here'" (Pace
1967: 581). Pace's findings suggest that the doorway to the
dayroom—as perceived by aides—symbolically marked the dayroom

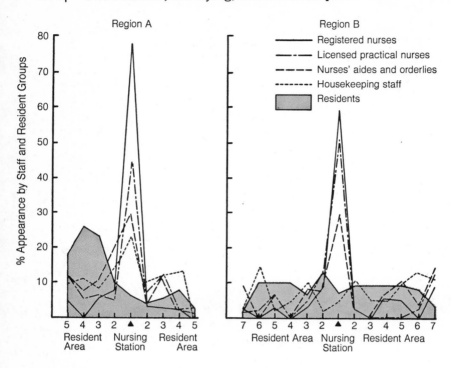

Distances Relative to the Nursing Station at which
Staff Appearances were Noted

Figure 5-1 VARIATIONS IN APPEARANCES OF DIRECT CARE
STAFF IN NURSING STATION AREAS IN THE REGIONS OF
EXTREMELY DISABLED ELDERLY (A) AND NONDISABLED
ELDERLY (B)

than their counterparts in the region of the nondisabled elderly.[2]
While the distribution modes in each region are in the nursing
station areas, a comparison of the graphs within floors and between
floors by staff status group reveals some differences whose implications are worthy of note.

For each residential region, staff status group appearances were
noted in the nursing station areas in the following rank order: (1)
Registered nurses were most frequently observed in or near the
nursing stations. Next were (2) licensed practical nurses, then (3)
nurses' aides and orderlies, then (4) housekeepers, who appeared
least in those areas. By statistical comparison, as shown in Table

ments and (2) the authority vested in nurses for decision making about the management of daily routines in each behavior region. Given these points, it is questionable whether the aide in Pace's study was representing (1) a supervisor-produced rationalization about the risk of upsetting "the boys back there"; or (2) the resistance of aides as a group to the risks of aggravating patients with illnesses of the types that characterized the dayroom group; or (3) impressions developed by aides, through sustained interactions with patients, about proper manners when dealing with members of the patient group.[3] In the last instance the distancing behavior could be symbolic of a rule about deportment developed through sustained interactions between aides and patients to ease their tension when in one another's presence (Le Bar 1964: 10, 14).

This interpretation of Pace's findings implies shared deliberations by staff and patients in selecting patterns of social ecological conduct. But such an interpretation does not apply in any straightforward fashion to the staff–patient relations reported in the present study. Deliberations between staff and patients about users and uses of places in a geriatric setting presuppose that members of each group have comparable access to information and comparable ability to process information about formal and informal codes of conduct. In a related study on levels of mental status among residents in the geriatric setting hosting the present study, residents in region A, unlike those in region B, had little or no ability to process information about daily routines and formal and informal codes for behavior. *Mental status* was conceived as the rank order of patients based on knowledge about their own social identity, knowledge about others, and knowledge about places and events in the settings of their daily routines.[4]

Considering the mental status of extremely disabled patients, Pace's implications for ecological arrangements based on shared systems of formal and informal rules must be modified, as follows. While the hypothesis of shared staff–patient deliberations seems reasonable with regard to region B where patients are relatively well and mentally alert, a hypothesis of staff-determined distributions seems more reasonable in region A, considering the mental status of residents. Those who lived in region A relied on staff to define regional proprieties as well as to provide servicing such as dressing, grooming, and toileting. Reasoning further, the inverse relation between the tails of the distributions of nursing staff and resident locations in region A (see Figure 5-3) is symbolic of socially sanctioned practices which minimize interactions between the physically and mentally well (nursing personnel) and the not-well (physically and mentally impaired elderly). Further observations of physical and behavioral constraints on movement in the severely disabled group helped to substantiate this line of reasoning.

Freedom and Behavioral Locks On the floor housing the severely impaired, the nursing station symbolized a lock beyond which most residents were not permitted to move. Several residents were physically turned back when they tried to walk beyond the station. The result was that most of the severely disabled were confined to the closed end of the corridor, whereas residents on the floor for the mildly disabled were more evenly distributed along the corridor (Figure 5-2).

It was also noted that several residents on the floor for the mildly disabled were regularly provided with walking aids such as canes and geriatric walkers, whereas no prosthetic devices were available on the floor for the severely disabled.

Further, it was obvious that although no physical constraints were placed on the movement or locomotion of the mildly disabled residents, the severely disabled residents were constrained in a variety of ways. The most common devices were geriatric chairs with tables locked across their arms. In addition, the single wheelchair available on the floor for the severely disabled was ordinarily immobilized, either because two loose spokes had been twisted around the axle or because the back rest had been tied to one of the hand rails along the wall. A final method of constraint involved simply fixing a cloth strap loosely across a resident's chest, effectively keeping the person seated when in an ordinary chair. The residents on whom such physical devices were used were found to be significantly lower in mental status than the unconstrained residents of the disabled floor (t = 3.8; p < .001).

In general, then, it was found that on the floor for the mildly disabled, residents were permitted to leave the unit at will, were provided with walking aids, and were not subjected to physical constraint. On the floor for the severely disabled, however, no residents were allowed to leave the unit unattended, and the majority were not permitted to move past the nurses' station. Finally, no resident of the severely disabled floor was provided with a walking aid.

Constraint Systems Certainly, most of the severely disabled residents were so disoriented that if permitted the use of the lounge they would be likely to leave the unit entirely and thereby violate the territorial preserves of others. It would hardly do to have them wandering around the bustling kitchen, the infirmary, or the morgue. Moreover, even the least impaired residents on the disabled floor had bad days, and on occasions they were retrieved from as far away as the surrounding neighborhoods outside the home. The need to restrict movement outside the unit is undeniable. Similarly, even if walking aids had been provided, many of the residents on the disabled floor were too impaired to use them. A cane is of little use to a resident who cannot understand its function or cannot stand up and walk in the first place.

Our interest here, however, is in the physical restrictions on the movement of the severely disabled. When questioned, staff members most frequently said that these restrictions were designed to prevent accidents. Without restraint, they said, residents would fall and injure themselves. This argument was no doubt valid when applied to many of the residents. But it does not explain the absence of walking aids for residents who *could* have used them, nor does it justify immobilization of the wheelchair. It would seem that there were other reasons, conscious or otherwise, underlying the system of constraints that we observed. Whatever the manifest intent of such restrictions, one of their effects was to impede or preclude the movement of residents through space even when there was no danger of injury.

It is clear that all the severely disabled residents were very low in mental status, and those who were systematically constrained were the lowest of all. The use of such constraints seems closely related to this low level of mental status, and the reasons for the use of constraints, aside from their legitimate protective value, are two. In the first place, territorial demands were just as operative on the disabled floor itself as they were elsewhere in the institution. Residents who are low in mental status apparently don't know where they are *not* supposed to be. They lack the capacity to understand territorial restrictions, occasionally shuffling into the nurses' station, or silently but physically intruding themselves into interactions between staff members or into staff–resident treatment situations. And since they do not recognize the symbols of territorial boundaries, the severely disabled cannot respond appropriately when staff members avert their faces, pointedly ignore them, or otherwise signal that a territorial violation has occurred.

A second reason for the imposition of restrictions seems to be the relative incapacity of the severely disabled for presenting a socially acceptable self. Severely disabled elderly are more likely than more competent residents to be mute, incontinent, and unkempt. Their speech and behavior are more likely to be bizarre, their thought processes less accessible, and their physical presence contaminating. Territorial intrusions that might be negotiated with a more competent person are likely to be seen by staff as unusually unpleasant.

In sum, highly disabled residents exhibit two social improprieties which result in their restraint. First, they do not understand the territorial demands of others in the institution. As a result, they fail to comprehend the system of interactional symbols through which territorial demands are expressed. Second, the severely disabled often lack the ability to project an image of integrated selfhood. The territorial boundaries inherent in organized social life are thereby even further strengthened against them. Restrictions imposed for such reasons are readily normalized since they exist in a geriatric setting where identical constraints are sometimes necessary for the physical safety of the residents.

None of these restrictions were placed upon residents living on the floor of the mildly disabled. In fact, their locomotion was implicitly encouraged through the provision of walking aids—because competent residents *know* when they are not wanted, and because they are *less often* not wanted. Staff-enforced physical constraint and highly restricted spaces for ambulation were replaced on the competent floor by shared recognition of territorial rights and by the ability of staff and residents to respond adaptively to one another's demands.

It is by means of our cooperative definition of proper conduct in socially symbolic spaces that we understand how to orient ourselves toward others by, say, maintaining the "correct" distance from them under a given set of circumstances. At the same time, we understand how to avoid transgressions into the territories of others, whether those others are present or not.

It may further be suggested that the processes outlined above, and discussed below, involve only two of several systems of constraint commonly found in custodial or rehabilitative institutions. There are other ways to regulate the movement of people through space, and any investigation of the problem must take into account at least the following systems, some of which are universal and some of which are not.

Physical object–constraint systems involve material artifacts, either fixed in space, like walls and other architectural features, or semifixed, such as furniture, doors, and movable screens (Hall 1969). *Fixed features* are not controvertible; and decisions about them, once made, are not easily revoked. The internal and external walls of a building, for example, help to determine the size and shape of rooms. In addition, the routes of passage to internal and external spaces and the arrangement of such objects as chairs and tables determine to a significant degree the variance in the flow of people as well as patterns in the uses of spaces within the establishment. Physical arrangements constituting the fixed features of space represent physical demands that must be met in an absolute sense as long as the features stand.

The constraints expressed in *semifixed features* are functional ones. The design and arrangement of tables and chairs, for example, may facilitate or inhibit interaction, but these limiting effects are not as unalterable as the effects of fixed-feature space. Traditionally, semifixed features have been designed in such a way as to be easily altered, as doors may be opened or closed.

Another means of control stems from *physical constraints dependent on psychopharmacological substances* available to staff in institutions charged with monitoring and treating severely ill people. Tranquilizers, sedatives, and hypnotics, as well as other drugs of which drowsiness is a side-effect, may be administered in order to keep disabled residents in their place. Although this may not be the stated intention, it is often the outcome.

The *application of physical devices*, instances of which have already been cited, constitutes another system of direct control that is perhaps more widely used than might be thought. The manipulation may be partial, as it is in the case of handcuffs, straitjackets, or the cast on a fractured limb. On the other hand, manipulation may involve the entire body of the patient. Whatever the devices, they represent an underlying system of *values among the socially well concerning proper appearances and movements* and a corresponding system of rules to guide actions that protect the system of values.

Finally, *consensual control* is a nonphysical system of constraints that requires neither objects around the body nor ingested substances. Rather, as we have already stated with regard to the floor housing mildly disabled elderly, consensual control is expressed in conventional behavior with respect to the definition and use of institutional space. As we shall see in the discussion of social reactions to severely disabled and dying persons, the social significance of these constraint systems aimed at regulating the behavior of severely disabled persons and controlling disabled–nondisabled interactions extends far beyond geriatric settings.

NEARNESS OF DEATH, DISTANCING BEHAVIOR, AND THE SEGREGATION OF PLACES FOR DYING

The physical ability to maintain oneself is only one measure by which the social acceptability of elderly persons is judged. Careful attention is also paid the mental status or competence of the elderly. Data collected with the Kahn–Goldfarb Mental Status Questionnaire (1961) and the Philadelphia Geriatric Center Checklist (Lawton 1971) revealed clear-cut differences in mental status between the severely disabled and the mildly disabled in the Jewish home ($t = 13.5$; $p < .001$). In other words, there was a positive correlation between physical and mental deterioration.

Given the finding that nursing stations and medical service offices function as backstage regions as well as dispensaries of professional services in geriatric settings, it is now hypothesized that residents with assigned bedrooms near medical service offices manifest lower mental impairment than residents assigned to bedrooms farther from the same offices. A high level of mental status was taken as a critical determinant of the residents' ability to articulate their needs for medical and paramedical services and to foster favorable impressions about themselves as cooperative patients. Given the nursing station as a backstage region for professional nurses, the permitted encroachments of elderly residents may signify the extent to which the social performances of the elderly, such as niceties in dress, talk, and ambulation, are consistent with social and institutional requirements for performance in service areas. The absence of the ability to articulate needs, as indicated by low mental status scores, was taken as a signifier of severe impairment and potential membership in a near-death group.

To help determine the relation between mental status and the distance of resident bedrooms from the medical service offices, a map was drawn of the floor area in the research ward which housed the severely disabled elderly (see Figure 5–4). The map shows nine subareas on the floor, with the nursing station as area "0" and four equidistant subareas extending the full length of the ward on each side of the station. Approximately five beds were located in each subarea. Our focus, however, was on patient appearances in the hallway, not in the bedrooms. For elderly members in each of the nine subareas, a mean mental status score was computed. Starting from a hunch that mean mental status scores were inversely related to distances of elderly subgroups from the nursing station, a

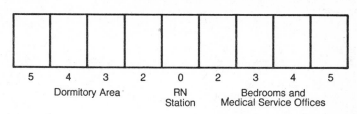

Figure 5-4 MAP OF THE FLOOR DIVISION OF THE RESEARCH WARD; NINE GRIDS HELP DEVELOP AN INVENTORY OF RESIDENT APPEARANCES BY SUBAREA LOCATION

determination was made of the relation between physical distance and the mean mental status score of each subgroup.

Mental Impairment, Residential Distance, and Near-Death Insignia Based on the Kahn–Goldfarb Mental Status Questionnaire (1961) and the Philadelphia Geriatric Center Checklist (1971), mental status was conceived as the rank order of residents as determined by the extent to which each could be distinguished from the other in terms of: (1) knowledge about social identity; (2) ability to identify others, such as service staff and family members who came to visit; and (3) knowledge about places and events inside and outside the home that were part of the context of the daily routines. It was found that the greater the distance of each subgroup from the nursing station and medical service offices, the lower the mean mental status score (see Figure 5-5). This finding was consistent with the hypothesis that low mental status would, in general, characterize elderly in the dormitory end of the ward as more severely disabled in interaction skills than those elderly assigned to bedrooms in the medical service area.

Official data on the incidence of subgroup (or subarea) mortalities provided further support for the inference that patients clustered in the dormitory area of the research ward could be thought of as a near-death group. The mortality data showed that 45 percent, or twenty members, of the group of forty-four residents living in the research ward at the beginning of the two-year period preceding this study were dead fifteen months later. Of those twenty deaths, eighteen, or 90 percent, occurred among residents assigned to the hypothetical subarea of the near-dead. While the mental status and mortality data suggest a close relationship between severity of illness and assignment to a room outside the nursing station area, these findings are not conclusive.

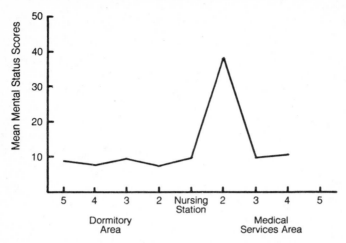

Resident Appearances by Rooms Assigned in
the Research Ward of the Jewish Home

Figure 5-5 RELATIONS BETWEEN MEAN MENTAL STATUS SCORES OF PATIENTS AND DISTANCES OF ASSIGNED BEDROOMS FROM MEDICAL SERVICE AREA

Further research is needed, focusing on psychological, demographic, and ecological indicators of social segregation in staff–resident interactions. In addition, decision-making processes among medical service staff should be taken into account. For example, Sudnow found that acts routinely performed by office, supervisory, and higher-ranking staff in general hospitals were so organized that staff systematically avoided more than incidental exposure to the dying and the dead (Sudnow 1967: 42–51). Other studies have shown that some hospitals are organized so as to concentrate the critically ill in a few wards where service is provided primarily by nursing assistants and orderlies (Blauner 1968: 535; Glaser and Strauss 1965: 535–536). Along with the selection of places for morgues and cemeteries, these patterns of interaction suggest a social structure which calls for the disengagement of high-ranking persons when there are signs that the demise of a group member is imminent. However, disengagement behavior may be less apparent or more reserved when the dying person occupies a high status, such as a political or religious leader. Nevertheless, it seems reasonable to expect distancing reactions among the living who anticipate that a particular individual is entering, irreversibly, into a state of death even before death-as-such is medically determined.

Despite the relative homogeneity of mental status in the area of the near-dead, the marked variations in the medical service area suggest that decline in mental status as such may not be as crucial a determinant as other factors in being allocated a place among the near-dead. One factor that might account for the distinction between subregional locations of near-dead residents and the sick—but less near-to-death—is conceptualized by Parsons as the behavior of actors who, when they show signs of illness, are accorded positions consistent with a "sick role" (Parsons 1951: 436–437).

Sick-role performance is defined by four criteria: (1) the individuals are exempted from such "normal social role responsibility" as self-care; (2) their condition requires physical and behavioral, "not merely attitudinal," change; (3) they "want to get well"; and, (4) they are willing to seek help and cooperate with technically competent others who can help them get well (Parsons 1972: 107, 117–118).

Distinguishing the Sick from the Near-Dead All the patients in the ward of the severely disabled elderly could easily qualify as sick actors on factors 1 and 2 of Parsons' schema. However, criteria 3 and 4 suggest that the legitimation of sickness is partly determined by the appropriateness of the illness behavior, as well as by the extent of medical and nursing staff conviction that the patient is qualified to enter into, or be retained in, a sick role.

When the movements and appearances of a patient no longer manifest the behaviors expected in a previously sustained helping relationship, medical and direct-care personnel may conclude that a sick-role classification and the getting-well-oriented behavior it implies may no longer apply to the disabled patient (Kassenbaum and Baumann 1972: 143–144; Twaddle 1969: 112–114; Ness 1973: 56). Stated another way: When professional health care workers decide that a patient is unable or unwilling to act in socially acceptable ways in a long-term care institution, it can be expected that the patient will be assigned a place among the irreversibly impaired. Or, depending on the extent of deterioration, the patient may be listed among the near-dead.

This is not to say that medical and nursing staff have precise techniques for reading, in the sequences of actions, the extent to which a patient has entered a near-death existence. The signs of illness may be too vague for a reading as precise as that. However, other near-death insignia may be perceptible to medical and nursing staff who have worked closely with patients for a long time. Fox (1957) provides some insights into this problem and process in her study of ways in which medical students are trained to cope with uncertainties in medical practice:

> The experience of being "on call" for an autopsy ("waiting around for someone to die") makes a student more conscious of the fact that, even when death is expected it is seldom wholly predictable. . . . Although ultimate death is certain, medical science is still not far enough advanced so that the physician can state with assurance exactly when an individual will die [Fox 1957: 216–217].

An excerpt from a study of "voodoo" death by Cannon, based on his analysis of a variety of anthropologists' records on the social organization of dying in South America, Africa, New Zealand, and elsewhere, suggests that the process of disengagement from the near-dead, as described in the foregoing, may in form be cross-culturally general, not institutionally specific.

> The doomed man is in a situation from which the only escape is by death. During the death-illness which ensues, the group acts with all the outreachings and complexities of its organization and with countless stimuli to suggest death positively to the victim who is in a highly suggestible state. In addition to social pressure upon him the victim himself, as a rule, not only makes no effort to live and to stay a part of his group but actually, through multiple suggestions which he received, cooperates in the withdrawal from it [Cannon 1958: 272].

So far as the foregoing reasoning is sound in its implications for the social organization of interactions with severely disabled elderly, further research should show that elderly patients in geriatric settings who are assigned to bedroom areas at varying distances from medical service offices will have had their assignments determined in part by their failure to meet the sick-role requirements of the gatekeepers for the well. Furthermore, geriatric staff, functioning as these gatekeepers, will, in assigning some elderly to near-death groups, have rendered a death-accelerating decision by disavowing the legitimacy of continuing to treat them as if they are sick, and not nearly dead. We will examine this conclusion further in chapter 7 when we consider the social structure of dying.

Summary and Conclusions

The first section of this chapter was devoted to a description of directly observable patterns in the use of space by nursing staff and patients in a home for the elderly. Primary attention was given to the behavior of staff users when they were in a region housing extremely disabled patients. For comparative purposes, nursing staff were also observed when they were in a region housing mildly impaired elderly.

It was expected that staff who delivered services to extremely disabled residents would manifest more clustering of their activities in places of refuge, such as nursing stations, rather than in primarily residential regions, thus reducing their interactions with residents. The findings were generally consistent with the hypothesized relationship between disability and staff uses of back regions, especially when comparing registered nurses and licensed practical nurses. Aides and orderlies showed no marked differences in uses of the nursing station areas when their behavior was compared in the regions of the severely disabled and the nondisabled elderly. Housekeeping staff did manifest more nursing station appearances in the region of the disabled than in the region of the nondisabled, but the differences could be accounted for by the presence of the housekeeper's utility room in the area of the nursing station in the region of the severely impaired. Since the utility room is in daily use, appearance of housekeeping staff in that area is in accord with their occupational obligations. By contrast, the storage closets in the region of the nondisabled were located at the ends of the corridors away from the nursing station.

Next, analysis was focused on observable patterns in the behavior of patient users in the two regions. It was expected that attempts by RNs and LPNs to minimize interaction with extremely disabled residents would be represented in observable concentrations of staff, not residents, in relatively distinct subregions of the floor housing the impaired elderly. The data from observations on the two floors yielded results generally consistent with the hypothesized relationships. Furthermore, the results show that the most highly trained nursing staff, presumably those groomed to service and guide the delivery of direct care for the elderly, are the least involved in the provision of direct care. In addition, the results suggested that highly trained staff engaged more frequently in interactions with and in servicing the least disabled patients, while leaving extremely disabled patients in the hands of lower-ranking staff.

This finding, which confirms previous research in this area, raises some serious questions about the raison d'être for extensive training of nurses who subsequently take positions in geriatric settings. If it is the least disabled patients and the managers of geriatric establishments who are the primary beneficiaries of the professional services rendered by upper status nursing staff, then nurses should be brought out from behind their uniform masks and made junior executives as their performances suggest they already are. This done, the actors who are now labeled nurses' aides, orderlies, and house-keepers could be given the status honors currently reserved for nurses—in view of the fact that nursing services are already the domain of aides and orderlies.

Finally, we saw that the elderly who manifested low levels of mental status but who retained places among the well patients, such as bedrooms in the medical service areas, may be understood as making favorable impressions on staff audiences. One of the crucial effects of continuing to foster favorable impressions in the gatekeepers of the nondisabled is to postpone the day of the patient's assignment to a place among the near-dead.

When (1) illness behavior reaches such extremes that it ceases to manifest characteristics that render to the sick an appearance of being in a temporary, not an irreversible, process of disability, and when (2) the patients begin to appear unresponsive or even reject attempts by others to intervene with procedures to reverse the illness, they may be removed from the visual and social presence of the well, including medical services. Segregating the severely mentally impaired from the well may have the effect of aggravating the condition of patients, especially those who have been chronically ill and have shown signs of mental disorientation. It was reasoned that the disengagement behavior of the well—as manifest in processes of segregation—will not only facilitate the breakdown of any remaining communication skills but will simultaneously accelerate the dying.

Against the background of these findings and interpretations, we now turn to a description of the internal order of a home for the black elderly. Analysis will focus on the similarities and differences between the two homes and the sociocultural implications.

Notes

1. These hours were selected in cooperation with the office of nursing and in light of the availability of assistant observers. Some nursing personnel on the evening shift in the region of the extremely disabled objected to the collection of data by scanning. One regional supervisor argued that the scanning procedure used in this study interrupted nursing activities and refused to be held responsible for what happened if

observations continued in the evening hours. It was then decided to limit all observations to the daytime hours.

2. The mean ($\overline{X}$) number of staff members per status group in each region for the first and second work shifts (7 A.M. to 3:30 P.M. and 3 to 11:30 P.M.) was as follows. Region A: RNs = 2; LPNs = 6; A/O = 8; and H = 3. Region B: RNs = 2; LPNs = 4; A/O = 7; and H = 3. To control for the influence of absolute numbers on the frequency at which members of any given subgroup were observed, the frequency scores per observation of subgroup members for each subarea in a region were divided by the mean number of staff on duty each day during the study. As such, the plotting points for the frequency polygons are based on the ratios of the frequencies of staff appearances in each regional subarea to the mean number of staff per status group on each floor during the six weeks of data collection.

3. In "Situational Therapy" Pace defined social organization as the shared system of formal and informal rules that join the physical milieux and routine uses of places as meaningful and significant contexts (Pace 1967: 581).

4. This concept of mental status is drawn from a conceptual analysis of the items in the extended form of the Mental Status Questionnaire partially developed and currently in use by M. Powell Lawton, Principal Investigator in a study of "Prosthetic Architecture for Mentally Impaired Aged," Philadelphia Geriatric Center, 1971.

References

Bennet, Ruth. "Social Context—A Neglected Variable in Research on Aging." *Aging and Human Development*, 1, 2 (1970), 97–116.

Blauner, Robert. "Death and Social Structure." In Bernice L. Neugarten, ed. *Middle Age and Aging*. Chicago: University of Chicago Press, 1968.

Blenkner, M. "Environmental Change and the Aging Individual." *The Gerontologist*, 7 (1967), 101–105.

Cahn, Edgar S., ed. *Our Brother's Keeper: The Indian in White America*. Washington, D.C.: New Community Press, 1969.

Cannon, Walter B. "Voodoo Death." In William A. Lessa and Evon Z. Vogt, eds. *Reader in Comparative Religion*. New York: Row, Peterson, 1958.

Chermayeff, Serge and Christopher Alexander. *Community and Privacy*. New York: Anchor Books, 1965.

Clark, Margaret. "The Anthropology of Aging: A New Area for Studies of Culture and Personality." *The Gerontologist*, 7, 1 (March 1967).

Fox, Renee C. "Training for Uncertainty." In Robert K. Merton, George Reader, and Patricia L. Kendall, eds. *The Student Physician*. Cambridge: Harvard University Press, 1957.

Glaser, Barney G., and Anselm L. Strauss. *Awareness of Dying*. Chicago: Aldine Press, 1965.

Goffman, E. *The Presentation of Self in Everyday Life*. New York: Doubleday-Anchor, 1959.

———. *Asylums*. New York: Anchor Books, 1961.

————. *Stigma: Notes on the Management of Spoiled Identity*. Englewood Cliffs, N.J.: Prentice-Hall, 1963.

Hall, E. T. *The Hidden Dimension*. Garden City, N.Y.: Doubleday–Anchor, 1969.

Henry, Jules. "Space and Power in a Psychiatric Unit." In Albert F. Wessen, ed. *The Psychiatric Hospital as a Social System*. Springfield, Ill.: Charles C. Thomas, 1964.

Kahn, R., M. Pollack, and A. Goldfarb. "Factors Related to Individual Differences in the Mental Status of Institutionalized Aged." In P. Hoch and J. Zubin, eds. *Psychopathology of Aging*. New York: Grune & Stratton, 1961.

Kassenbaum, Gene G., and Barbara O. Baumann. "Dimensions of the Sick Role in Chronic Illness." In E. Gartley Jaco, ed. *Patients, Physicians and Illness*. New York: Free Press, 1972.

Lawton, M. P. "Prosthetic Architecture for Mentally Impaired Aged." Unpublished summary and progress report, Philadelphia Geriatric Center, Philadelphia, 1971.

Le Bar, Frank M. "Some Implications of Ward Structure for Enculturation of Patients." In Albert F. Wessen, ed. *The Psychiatric Hospital as a Social System*. Springfield, Ill.: Charles C. Thomas, 1964.

Lieberman, M. A. "Relationship of Mortality Rates to Entrance to a Home for the Aged." *Geriatrics*, 16 (1961), 515–519.

Maxwell, R. J., J. E. Bader, and W. H. Watson. "Territory and Self in a Geriatric Setting." *The Gerontologist*, 12, 4 (Winter 1972), 413–417.

Ness, Katherine M. "The Sick Role of the Elderly." In Irene M. Burnside, ed. *Psychosocial Nursing Care of the Aged*. New York: McGraw-Hill, 1973.

Neugarten, Bernice L., ed. *Middle Age and Aging*. Chicago: University of Chicago Press, 1968.

Pace, Robert E. "Situational Therapy." *Journal of Personality*, 25 (1967).

Parsons, Talcott. *The Social System*. New York: Free Press, 1951.

————. "Definitions of Health and Illness in the Light of American Values and Social Structure." In E. Gartley Jaco, ed. *Patients, Physicians and Illness*. New York: Free Press, 1972.

Sommer, Robert. *Personal Space*. Englewood Cliffs, N.J.: Prentice-Hall, 1969.

Sudnow, David. *Passing On*. Englewood Cliffs, N.J.: Prentice-Hall, 1967.

Twaddle, Andrew C. "Health Decisions and Sick Role Variations: An Exploration." *Journal of Health and Social Behavior*, 10, 2 (June 1969), 106–114.

Watson, Wilbur H. "Body Idiom in Social Interaction: A Field Study of Geriatric Nursing." Unpublished doctoral dissertation, Department of Sociology, University of Pennsylvania, Philadelphia, 1972.

SOCIAL INTERACTION IN A HOME FOR THE BLACK ELDERLY | 6

In the previous chapter, which studied the elderly in a Jewish home and their relationship with the staff, severity of physical and mental impairment was shown to be closely related to the disengagement of medical and paramedical personnel from care and service. Also observed, but unreported, was the fact that the home for the Jewish elderly had an all-white patient population but a racially mixed staff. Considering the racial homogeneity of the residents and the racially mixed staff, it seems worthwhile to explore the extent of similarity in the social structures of the Jewish home and other homes that differ in race of residents and staff.

To explore the significance of race in the social structure of health care and social interaction with the elderly, a home for the elderly was selected for study with a resident population of 174, 98 percent of them black, and a predominantly black staff of health care personnel. Our general hypothesis is as follows: The "color line" (Du Bois 1903; 1947) has been institutionalized as a symbol of group differences and rules for social interaction in America. This implies corresponding differences between black and white people in values and rules for reacting to infirm members of groups observably or socially associated with the other side of the color line. So far as it is reasonable to regard socially defined Jewish people as a white American ethnic group and socially defined Africans in America as a black American ethnic group (Kitano 1974; Sklare 1971), we seek in this chapter to determine the extent of observable similarities and differences between traditional approaches to health care and face-to-face interaction with infirm elderly members of each group. Our aim is to isolate the differences and describe similarities in reactions to infirm Jewish and black elderly persons.

We acknowledge that an in-depth and comparative analysis of the histories of Jewish and black American ethnic groups, including social definitions of race and traditional relations between the elderly and their keepers, would be most conducive to a full understanding of any observed differences. However, this study is exploratory. We aim to formulate questions for further research about ethnic variations in aging and social reactions to aging, rather than pretend to reach conclusions about these variations. To facilitate insight, we have elected to focus on the social structures of interactions between Jewish and black American elderly and their keepers in nursing homes.

The research settings were two relatively modern homes for the elderly. The Jewish home was described in the previous chapter. Since we are particularly interested in social reactions to the physical and mental impairments of old age, our focus is primarily on structural differences and similarities in staff interactions with the severely disabled.

Behavior Regions in the Black Home for the Aged

The black home for the aged, like the Jewish home, had a full range of elderly residents varying in ability to dress, feed, toilet, and otherwise maintain themselves. Furthermore, each home was part of a full geriatric center or multiservice institution. The range of health, social service, dietary, and other professionals in each home made it possible for the administrators to offer a variety of services to a variety of elderly persons, from those capable of relatively independent living to those who were extremely disabled and highly dependent. To determine the bearing of physical and mental disability on interactions between the elderly and their keepers, we selected for observation one group representing the extremely disabled and one group representing the relatively nondisabled in each home. In addition to interactions between the elderly and health care personnel, we wanted to determine the extent to which the relations between disabled elderly and the spaces assigned to them in the Jewish home were similar to the relations between the disabled and the staff in the black home.

A Comparison of Resident Populations in the Black and Jewish Homes for the Elderly

There were 174 residents of the black home during the period of this study—137 (79 percent) females and 37 (21 percent) males. Ages in the black home ranged from 60 to 100 years, with a mean of 80 years.

The full population of the Jewish home was 328 residents during the eleven months of the study. Of the 328 residents, 256 (78 percent) were females and 72 (22 percent) were males at any given point in time. Ages of residents in the Jewish home ranged from 59 to 104 years, with a mean of 83 years. The two homes, then, were very similar in both proportion of sexes and age range.

SEVERELY DISABLED RESIDENTS OF THE TWO HOMES

In the black home 37 residents, 4 male and 33 female, lived in the region of the severely disabled. These residents, all black, had a mean age of 79 years. In physical self-maintenance, 67 percent could walk unaided between their rooms and dining areas, lounges, and offices of professional services on the floors where they lived. While 33 percent of these residents required canes, walkers, or staff assistance for long-distance ambulation, geriatric chairs were much less in evidence here than they were in the region for the severely disabled at the Jewish home. Furthermore, 43 percent of the severely disabled black elderly were incontinent and 70 percent required assistance in dressing and grooming. About 65 percent of the disabled black elderly could feed themselves without assistance.

Mental status was measured for each resident by the combined ratings of nurses and social workers on a checklist representing their judgments that a resident was competent, somewhat competent, often incompetent, or incompetent. Of the residents in the ward for the severely disabled black elderly 70 percent were rated as incompetent. The idea of resident incompetence was similar in the black home and in the Jewish home.

The Social Structure of Architectural Regions and Uses of Space

To facilitate a comparison of the black home for the elderly with findings reported about the Jewish home, we began with interviews of nurses, social workers, and administrators at the black home. The interviews were intended to provide insight into the factors helping to determine administrative decisions in assigning residents to particular bedrooms and activity areas. They would enable us to compare the assignment of space to residents in the black home and in the Jewish home. Interviews were supplemented by direct observation of residential regions or wards, frequency and quality of interaction between nursing personnel and elderly residents, and the frequency of personnel appearances in nursing stations, staff lounges, and other places specifically set aside for nursing personnel.

The interview data collected at the black home revealed that, after admission to the home, a decline in walking, grooming, bathing, feeding, and toileting was commonly accompanied by an administrative decision to move the resident into a subregion designed for the care of the severely disabled. In this respect, the two homes were structurally similar.

Data on the incidence of mortality among the thirty-seven members of the severely disabled group in the black home showed that the five (14 percent) who died during the 12 months preceding this study were diagnostically incompetent, and they had been housed in a relatively remote subregion of the ward whose elderly members were similar to those characterized in the Jewish study as a near-death group. Subregions 2 to 4 in Figure 6–1 illustrate what could be called the subregion of the near-dead in the home for the black elderly. The severely impaired residents in the near-death groups generally showed the most extreme mental incompetence as well as severe physical disability, and their prognoses suggested that further medical intervention would not significantly alter their physical or mental condition. As already shown in the chapter on the Jewish home, there was a positive association between staff attitudes and resident assignments to bedrooms close to nursing stations. In other words, nurses tended to surround their offices with residents who required the least assistance in dressing, eating, walking, and toileting; whose constraint in ambulation kept to a minimum their trespassing on staff territory; and whose appearances and approaches to staff members were, by implication, least likely to offend the character ideals they cherished.

Observations of staff–resident intereaction and bedroom assignment in the black home, as shown in Figure 6–1 and later in Table 6–1, indicate a practice significantly different from the Jewish home. Nursing stations and nurse interventions in patient affairs seemed

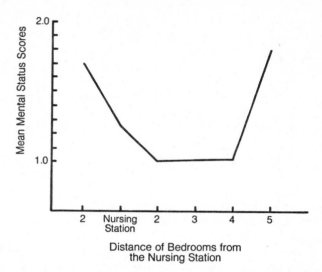

Figure 6-1 MEAN MENTAL STATUS AND DISTANCE OF RESI-DENT BEDROOMS FROM NURSING SUBSTATION IN WARD FOR SEVERELY DISABLED ELDERLY BLACKS*

*The points on the curve were found by the following procedure: Each resident occupying a bedroom on the floor was assigned a score of 2 if rated high in mental status (or mental competence), and a score of 1 if rated incompetent, as judged by nursing and social service staff. Then, extending in each direction down the corridor from the nursing station, relatively equidistant grids were marked off by every second bedroom door. This procedure permitted a distinction between four subbedroom regions in one direction and one subregion in the other direction, with the bedrooms in the nursing station constituting region one (see Figure 5-5 for a similar demarcation of subregions based on observations in the Jewish home). To find the average competence score for residents in each subregion of the black home, the sum of the values, 2 and 1, assigned to competent and incompetent residents was divided by the number of residents for that subregion. This produced a set of mean scores, ranging from 1.0 to 1.75. It is the relation between mean mental status scores and subregional distances from the nursing station that constitutes the data bases for this figure.

more frequently aimed at the severely disabled, with the mildly disabled more frequently left to fend for themselves. Implications of this finding are discussed in further detail in a section on social class and ethnic differences in reactions to disabled elderly.

Architecturally, the subregions for the severely impaired in the . two homes were in areas physically invisible from the main entrances and corridors. As already noted, these social and architectural arrangements are generally consistent with findings from other studies focused on the internal order of specialized institutions that care for severely disabled persons (Sudnow 1967; Glaser and Strauss 1965; Blauner 1968; Watson 1974).

Rules for Appearances in Public Places

Lining corridors flowing inward from the main entrances to the black and the Jewish homes for the elderly were the relatively well or nondisabled residents. These are persons who can walk with little or no assistance, who are sufficiently alert to recognize and exchange greetings with staff or visitors, and who can on occasion be observed carrying on conversations. In this we see another similarity between the two homes.

The observable distinctions in the behavior of elderly persons permitted to appear in relatively public places and those restricted to back regions or secluded places suggest the following: When socially disreputable appearance and behavior develop in human groups, the socially inept are assigned to places where they are less visible to the physically and mentally unblemished members of the society. Excluding the extremely disabled from places that permit scrutiny of their failings protects the nondisabled from exposure to human frailties that are or will be their own through imminent senescence.

This interpretation of patterned segregation of severely disabled elderly fits in with Foucault's analysis of the history of social reactions to leprosy and other forms of physical and mental deviance, with special focus on the Age of Reason. Especially germane to our discussion is Foucault's observation of the persistence of social exclusion as a way of coping with group members who no longer perform publicly in ways that reinforce socially sanctioned values. Note, for example, the following observation about the social historical significance of places set aside to house socially rejected persons:

> Often, in these places, the formulas of exclusion would be repeated, strangely similar two or three centuries later. Poor vagabonds, criminals, and "deranged minds" would take the part played by the leper . . . With an altogether new meaning and in a very different culture, the forms would remain essentially that major form of a rigorous division which is social exclusion [Foucault 1965: 68].

Along with the cross-ethnic generality in human reactions to severely disabled members of groups, Foucault's study and others

(Sigerist 1943; Rosebury 1969) indicate the historical depths of these patterns of adaptation. As we discuss in a later chapter on the social structure of dying, exclusion of the severely disabled may be the ritual reaction of primate groups to severely disabled members, however culturally variable in expression. Given the consistency between administrators of the homes in physically and visually excluding the disabled from daily contact with the nondisabled, we can now compare the two homes with a focus on similarities and differences between the internal structures of places or subregions set aside to house the severely disabled elderly.

Mental Status and Social Behavior

Within the context of places set aside for the severely disabled, beds for patients were commonly located in large dormitory rooms stripped of doors and movable bedside screens by which the elderly residents could achieve privacy. One explanation for the absence of architectural arrangements that would permit residential privacy was offered by the director of social service in the home for the black elderly:

> Residents should have ways of achieving privacy when they want it, especially when dressing, bathing, or toileting themselves. But when they get badly confused, it doesn't matter too much if they are put in dormitory rooms like the ones that we have in this home.

While this statement is clear on the surface, its implications suggest a question about the criteria by which professional staff identify a person as badly confused. This may be thought of as the problem of "confusion–determinism" (Watson 1974). Professional judgment about the extent of mental impairment in an elderly resident is unquestionably a significant factor in determining the kind of care to be planned and implemented. However, there is often ambiguity in the processes by which these decisions are made. Intrastaff disagreement about signs of health or illness in the behavior of patients is common. While self-maintenance abilities—particularly walking, feeding, toileting, and dressing—are important determinants of the health status assigned to the elderly by their keepers, mental competence remains an important criterion in its own right.

Within the subregions of the severely disabled, exploratory observations of the locations-of-activities of ambulatory/articulate and nonambulatory/articulate residents suggested that the sorting of patients by severity of illness between subresidential regions was not limited to determining their assignment to geriatric wards. Instead, the process of sorting the well from the not-well and sifting out the sick from the near-dead extended into the face-to-face interactions and the uses of space within the regions set aside for the severely disabled. The data whose analyses helped to reveal this were drawn from an exploratory study of the relation between mental status of the patients assigned to bedrooms in or near the medical service areas and those assigned to rooms in the subregions of the severely disabled in both the Jewish and the black homes for the elderly.

To ascertain the relationship between low mental status and proximity to medical service offices in the black home, the identifying numerals for resident bedrooms in each research setting were arranged into an array with the nursing station in each region treated as zero distance in the array. Following a determination of the mental status of each resident, as measured by two or more staff ratings, the data for residents rating low were sorted and compared by bedroom location. It was expected that the lower the rating, the greater the observed distance between the bedroom and the nursing station on the floor. The frequency distributions of residents distinguished by mental status and distance from the nursing stations in the Jewish and black homes are presented in Table 6-1.

The table shows that a greater proportion of severely disabled elderly were assigned rooms far from, rather than near, the nursing stations in each home. However, there were significantly more elderly in the far group of the Jewish home than in the corresponding group of the black home ($t = 6.17$, p $< .0005$).

Table 6-1 MENTAL IMPAIRMENT OF RESIDENTS BY LOCATION OF BEDROOMS IN THE SUBREGIONS OF THE SEVERELY DISABLED IN THE JEWISH AND THE BLACK HOMES FOR THE ELDERLY

Distance from Medical Service Offices	Jewish Home	Black Home
Near	18%	41%
Far	82%	59%
N	28	26

*The comparisons represented by this table are based solely on the total number of elderly in the research wards of each home who were rated "often incompetent" and "incompetent."

In a previous study (Watson 1974) it was reasoned that widespread concentrations of mentally impaired elderly in locations far removed from health service offices in specialized settings could be symbolic of general cross-cultural patterns of social reactions to the severely disabled. The ultimate assignment of extremely disabled elderly to places for the near-dead, such as geriatric wards populated by mentally incompetent and frequently incontinent elderly, signifies their failure to meet the sick-role requirements of the gatekeepers for the well.

It could be argued that Table 6–1 represents social reactions to disabled elderly who fail the sick-role test. However, social relations between the disreputable elderly and their keepers are, or may be, characterized by ethnic nuances within the broad social-historical patterns of exclusion described in this book. As suggested in the following discussion of social class and status parity in structures of social interaction, there may be ethnic differences that influence definitions of illness and dying, as well as qualitative differences between ethnic groups in face-to-face interactions with their disabled members.

Social Class and Ethnic Differences Between Homes for the Elderly

The distribution of mental status scores by location of resident bedrooms in the wards of the two homes was in general consistent with the hypothesis that residents with low mental status would show disproportionate clustering in primarily residential areas and away from the area of the medical service offices. The percentage distributions in Table 6–1 for the Jewish home and the black home manifest a pattern consistent with this hypothesis. However, the different proportions of Jewish and black elderly in the far room areas of the respective wards warrant further inquiry.

STATUS PARITY AND SOCIAL REACTIONS TO THE SEVERELY DISABLED AND DYING ELDERLY

A reexamination of the data describing the resident populations of each setting, as displayed in Table 6–2, showed that the Jewish home and the black home differed significantly in socioeconomic class characteristics of their respective residents ($x^2 = 64.9$, 1 df; $p < .0001$). Although few details about specific features of the homes were available at the writing of this report, it was established that, of

Table 6-2 CLASS DIFFERENCES BETWEEN RESIDENTS BY
PROPORTIONS IN EACH OF TWO HOMES WHO CAN
AFFORD TO PAY FOR PART OR ALL OF THE
COSTS OF LONG-TERM CARE

Class Differences	*Types of Homes*	
	JEWISH	BLACK
Haves*	98%	75%
Have Nots†	2%	25%
N	328	190

*Proportion of residents who can pay for part or all of their long-term care.
†Proportion of residents who cannot pay for any part of long-term care.

the 328 residents of the Jewish home, 98 percent had private financial means to help pay the costs of their care; only 2 percent of the 328 were totally dependent on Old Age Assistance (OAA). By contrast, 75 percent of the 190 residents in the black home at the inception of this study had private financial means to help pay the costs of their care.[1] Fully 25 percent of the residents in the black home were altogether dependent on OAA.

Further comparisons showed that the black home, unlike the Jewish home, was severely understaffed as far as professional nursing personnel were concerned. The care of the residents in the black home was basically in the hands of aides and orderlies under the supervision of licensed practical nurses. Like the lower-order staff whose location-activity inventories showed greater proportions of time in primarily residential areas when compared to upper status nursing staff in the Jewish home (see Figures 5-1, 5-2, and 5-3), observations of location-activity inventories of aides and orderlies in the black home showed similar distributions in the behavior of lower status staff.

Lower status nursing personnel—most of them black, and most of them manifesting social class characteristics similar to those of their elderly charges in the black home—can be thought of as engaged in race-related and economic status parity relations when serving most of the residents they contact in the black home. Status parity here means a similarity in socially defined rank and honor when compared to a standard system of values whose objects or attributes they possess in varying amounts. Social definitions of race in America and socioeconomic attributes of class, such as level of income, education, and property ownership, are not the only variables in determining status parity. Chronological age, sex, esthetic appearance, and health are other important determinants of social status.

Recent studies support the significance of status parity as a determinant of extroversion in social relations: (1) Rosow found (1965) that elderly persons are more socially outgoing in communities of elders than they are in age-integrated settings; (2) Watson found (1970; 1974; 1975) that youthful, able-bodied geriatric nurses show preferences for interaction with their nondisabled patients rather than disabled elderly; (3) other observations[2] show that, in matters of health status, the relatively well elderly residents in the Jewish home expressed preferences for common residence and interaction with other nondisabled elderly rather than having the disabled among them. These studies and others (Aguilera 1967; Worcester 1961) point to the significance of analyzing status parity as a variable in selective interaction.

Black nursing staff, especially lower status staff such as aides and orderlies, and black lower class elderly may sense a strong bond through their common plight in a society that punishes people for being black and lower class. Their tendency to interact with each other more than with persons who differ from them in race and socioeconomic class can be interpreted as a signifier of social solidarity and of sentiments they hold in common. This means that when black lower class staff are largely responsible for servicing black lower class residents in homes for the elderly, it is reasonable to expect more approach than avoidance behavior between them than between people who share neither race nor class parity.

If this reasoning holds, interactions between white nursing staff and white elderly residents who share a common socioeconomic status should also reveal more approach than avoidance behavior. Unfortunately, we did not have access to a home with predominantly white staff and residents and so were unable to assess the merits of this hypothesis. However, the findings from the studies of the Jewish and the black homes suggest research in this direction.

Observed Differences in Staff–Resident Interaction in the Jewish and the Black Homes

In the research wards of both the Jewish and the black homes, the nursing staff were predominantly black. Table 6-3 illustrates the

Table 6-3 PERCENTAGES OF BLACK NURSING PERSONNEL ON THE DAY SHIFT (8 A.M. TO 4 P.M.) FOR COMPARABLE FLOORS IN THE JEWISH AND THE BLACK HOMES FOR THE ELDERLY

Types of Nursing Personnel	Jewish Home		Black Home	
	TOTAL STAFF	% BLACK	TOTAL STAFF	% BLACK
Registered nurses	4	50%	2	50%
Licensed practical nurses	10	80%	2	100%
Nurses' aides	12	100%	7	100%
Orderlies	3	100%	1	100%
N	29		12	

distributions of nursing personnel by status and race in selected wards of the two homes. The table clearly shows that the nursing personnel were overwhelmingly black in each home.

In accordance with the hypothesized influences of status parity on social interaction, it is reasonable to expect that white personnel in the Jewish home will be less restrained and more expressive than black personnel when interacting with white elderly residents. Table 6-4 compares the frequency of instrumental and expressive touching of Jewish elderly initiated by black and white staff in the Jewish home.

Expressive touching reflects a sense of freedom to display affection for the person with whom interaction occurs. By contrast, instrumental touching is essentially an act to facilitate the achievement of another goal—such as wrist holding while helping a resident to walk (Watson 1975). Instrumental acts are explained by the institutional and occupational structures which shape their expression. In

Table 6-4 INSTANCES OF INSTRUMENTAL AND EXPRESSIVE TOUCHING INITIATED BY BLACK AND WHITE NURSING STAFF IN A HOME FOR THE JEWISH ELDERLY

Types of Touching	Race of Initiator	
	WHITE	BLACK
Expressive	58%	25%
Instrumental	42%	75%
N	41	147

a fully functioning institutional structure, status parity should have little or no effect on instrumental acts, unless status parity is itself required by the structure. However, expressive behavior varies independently of institutional constraints (Watson 1975) and is more sensitive to personal and interpersonal variables.

Table 6-4 clearly shows that white nursing personnel engaged in significantly more expressive interactions, while black personnel showed a preponderance of instrumental touching in interactions with white elderly Jewish residents (x^2 = 16.283, df = 1; p < .001). If we consider racial identity as a status variable, as it is in a racially stratified society like the United States—then examine race-related parity as represented between a white nurse and patient, or a black nurse and patient as we have done in this study—we would have, in each case, instances of high race-related status parity. This does not mean that status parity is the only important factor that may help to explain the relations between them. There are, of course, other important variables that can influence touching and other behavior. Included among them are the self-imagery and sociocultural backgrounds of the persons. For example, even under conditions of parity, black and/or white interaction partners may not prefer to be saturated with each other's company, at least publicly. Each may be influenced in the choice of interaction partners and expressive behavior by extra-ethnic factors, such as pressures for "racial integration," that may propel them away from each other and toward their racial opposites. Same sex and dissimilar sex pairs, age differences, physical stigma, and a variety of psychological factors may also exert important influences. However, our aim in this study was limited. We sought, through the available data, to examine the significance of status parity as it arose through our successive formulation of hypotheses and analyses carried out in the field. We did not intend an exhaustive study of ethnic variations in expressive touching. The finding shown in Table 6-4 is generally consistent with the hypothesized effect of status parity on social interaction, and geriatric health care in particular. In sum, the greater the degree of parity that one person perceives or imagines between his status in a group and that of another person, the greater the likelihood of expressive interaction between them.

There were too few white members of the nursing staff (N = 2) and too few observations of staff behavior in the black home to permit a status parity analysis there.[3] However, there were slivers of qualitative data from each home which, in substance, suggested other race-related variations in staff interactions with residents.

A black licensed practical nurse (LPN) at the Jewish home revealed through interviews that she and other black staff found it difficult to form cordial relations with their Jewish charges. She reported that some Jewish residents periodically expressed race-related. hostility toward black staff. As a long-term consequence, it became routine for established black members of the nursing staff to limit themselves to instrumental interactions with most residents. The following instance, as described by the LPN, is illustrative of alienating acts of white elderly residents:

> Many of these residents don't like Negroes. A male resident told me, "You should've stayed slaves."
>
> I complained to the supervisor yesterday that he called me a nigger, slut, and all kinds of other things when I tried to pass medicine. The supervisor came down and looked, but she did nothing until the resident tried to hit me with a steel cane. Then, she reprimanded him and tried to quiet him down.

In this instance the resident's hostility toward the nurse interfered with the nurse's effort to complete the instrumental act of passing medicine. For the severely disabled elderly man who expressed racist hostility toward the nurse, his problem was more serious and complex than that implied in his expressed concern about being with blacks no longer restricted to the fields and mansions of a plantation economy. The rejected black person was in fact a skilled nurse whose competence in health care procedures was essential to the patient's biopsychological sustenance. Furthermore, the nurse was one of several whose judgment that the patient was cooperative would decide whether his treatment continued as a member of the sick, not the nearly-dead. By his race-related anger, expressed through hostility toward the black licensed practical nurse, this white patient was clearly endangering his own life chances by cutting off a significant source of professional health care. More than likely the patient was not totally aware of this situation as analyzed.

As expected, following the hypothesis of race-related status parity, in the home for the black elderly no black LPNs reported the kinds of abuse and the subsequent feelings of alienation expressed in the aforementioned incident.

Another difference in relations between staff and elderly was evident in the black home, where nursing personnel and elderly observed joking relations about institutional and noninstitutional matters. By contrast, joking relations with residents in the Jewish home seemed limited to interactions with white staff. However, black staff members in the Jewish home did engage in considerable joking and playful interactions among themselves.

Finally, some observations were made of staff relations with residents in each home who were diagnostically classified as incontinent. An incontinent patient eliminates urine and feces in unconventional places and could even take to smearing bodily wastes over the surface of the body or on lavatory walls, bedroom walls, or other surfaces (Stanton and Schwartz 1954: 367). Although we did not systematically investigate the social-psychological aspects of incontinence, a few closing comments are warranted on qualitative observations.

As described in chapter 5, geriatric chairs and other physical constraint systems were conspicuous in the ward housing the severely disabled Jewish elderly. We inferred from our observations there that carefully constrained or limited spatial mobility of incompetent/ambulatory residents was favored over permitting residents to walk or move about in wheelchairs, although their walking might be aimed at getting to a lavatory for conventional evacuation of bodily wastes. This does not mean that staff deliberately or consciously interfered with toileting behavior; it *does* mean that physical constraints on the spatial mobility of incompetent persons has the effect, albeit inadvertent, of preventing socially acceptable waste elimination.

However, other factors also help to explain the incidence of incontinence. Obviously, a person has to have enough mental competence and psychomotor coordination to sense gastrointestinal changes and respond to organic pressures that signal a need for waste elimination. In fact, increases in the incidence of incontinence clearly corresponded with increasing mental incompetence for any given ward in both homes. Less obvious but no less significant here is an earlier study by Stanton and Schwartz (1954: 366–377) focused on incontinence in mental hospitals. Five social factors or elements of staff–patient relations were found associated with the incidence of incontinence among patients:

1. *Conflict.* When there was general disturbance or excitement on a ward, such as is generated by open conflict between staff about lines of authority in hospital management, labor–management relations, or proprieties in the management of patient behavior, incontinence increased. Patient failure in competition with other patients was also associated with incontinence.

2. *Abandonment.* When patients were denied opportunities to participate in group activities on and off a ward, or when a previously rewarding relationship with a staff member or patient was dissolved, incontinence increased.
3. *Isolation.* This factor is closely related to abandonment. It is represented when a patient is ignored or treated as an outsider by other patients and staff with whom a sustained social relationship had existed or had been anticipated.
4. *Devaluation.* This phenomenon is represented when a patient is blamed for something—perhaps done by someone else; or when a patient is made the butt of another person's critical or contemptuous remarks or gestures. Devaluation contributes to a loss of self-esteem.
5. *Unconstructive situation.* This phenomenon represents poor judgment by staff in planning patient activities. It entails denial of an opportunity to participate at the level of the patient's capabilities or stage of psychosocial development.

In regard to unconstructive situations, patient self-evaluations may be higher than their social or staff evaluations. Under these circumstances, staff may frequently, albeit unwittingly, err in their professional judgments and planning for patients and indirectly engender incontinence by not taking into account the patients' own self-imagery about their social skills. In general, the Stanton and Schwartz findings are provocative. They show that incontinence can be triggered by an intricate complex of biological, psychological, and social factors.

In fact, we were informed by two licensed practical nurses in the black home about a practice they implemented, together with some nurses' aides, where they closely observed residents who were diagnostically incompetent and who, if left to their own resources, could be expected to be actively incontinent. The nurses instituted an increased number of inspection tours in the ward of the severely disabled with the intent of taking them to the lavatories. The result was significantly less recorded incontinence (43 percent) in wheelchairs, bedrooms, and other unconventional places. In contrast, 83 percent incontinence was reported for a similar disability group in the Jewish home. These differences in the incidence of incontinence between the severely disabled in the Jewish and the black homes occurred even though the proportions of elderly rated incompetent were nearly identical—66 and 70 percent respectively.

In conjunction with the results of previous research (Stanton and Schwartz 1954; Maxwell et al, 1972; Watson 1972), these findings clearly show the need for careful studies of interactional determinants of incontinence. Our own results have shown a relation between the quality of face-to-face interaction and the incidence of incontinence. The observed differences between the two homes were sufficient to justify the initiation of further inquiry.

Summary: The Need for Comparative Studies of Aging in Institutional Settings

Status-related class differences in perceptions of aging and in the organization of behavior in the care of the elderly have been shown to be important factors in the institutionalization of aging and dying. Some groups in the United States exalt the virtues of youth and youthful appearances of the human body. But in other groups the presence of suffering, signs of aging and dying, disability, and status deprivation may lead to deference and face-to-face interaction rather than . distancing and nonperson treatment. Interaction is especially likely when the caretakers share with the elderly a common class and/or ethnic background (Wax 1961; Cahn 1969; Watson 1971).

Comparative studies are needed of individual and collective behavior in different regions within institutional settings (Bennet 1970). We have already seen in our comparisons of the Jewish and the black home some evidence of similarities and differences in staff–patient interaction when the extent of the physical disability of residents is varied. We also showed that the social significance of subinstitutional settings differed with the use of the settings to house the well and the dying, and that such differences are built into the architectural arrangements of the settings. While there have been previous studies of behavior regions and setting analyses (Goffman 1959; 1961; 1963; 1964; Barker 1961a; 1961b; 1963; 1968; Willems 1965; Sudnow 1967), few of these studies have been focused specifically on institutional settings for the elderly. The ongoing studies of Lawton and associates on prosthetic architecture for the mentally impaired aged (1971) and the recent collection of papers by Pastalan and Carson (1970) are notable exceptions.

The relations between mortality and admissions of the elderly to settings specialized for their care is another area in which there has been a shortage of research. A number of studies have documented sharp increases in mortality rates of elderly following change of residence—for example, when moving from a private residence into a home for the elderly (Blenkner 1967; Lieberman 1961; Lawton 1970). The mortality rates, variously referred to as signifiers of "admissions trauma" and "transplantation shock," point to the need to focus on health differences and other individual characteristics that may distinguish survivors from nonsurvivors during the first year following admission to a specialized setting. Chronic brain syndrome has been suggested as an important factor for further study in relation to admissions trauma (Blenkner 1967; Lieberman 1961). Lawton and Yaffe (1970) have suggested the importance of further research focused on the extent to which individual choice is a factor codeterminant with chronic brain syndrome that may help to explain admissions trauma.

Furthermore, preadmissions differences in social class, the importance assigned to permanence as against change in the order of things, and advantageous life-styles may help to differentiate survivors from nonsurvivors (Riley, Johnson, and Foner 1971). For example, low income black inner city elderly have always known unemployment and changes of residence, and they secured life-sustaining resources such as food, shelter, and clothing through daily struggles in a harsh social environment. This conditioning may allow for a higher survival rate than members of other groups in the first months after admission to a home, hospital, or other specialized setting for the elderly.

Clearly, then, aging and dying in specialized institutions, as in society at large, are processes about which many questions remain unanswered. Principal among the factors requiring more systematic study are (1) social definitions of physical and mental impairment and (2) the social organization of caretakers who service the disabled and dying elderly.

There is also a need for studies of the professionals and paraprofessionals who work in the service of the elderly. In particular, we need to focus on differences in training, age, sex, race, ethnicity, language, and other social, cultural, and personality factors that may exist among professional staff and their assistants that may influence the relations developed with the elderly they are intended to serve.

Discussions throughout this section focused on the policy implications of research on specialized institutions for the elderly. In addition to further research on the relations between architectural arrangements and the social organization of disability groups and caretaker behavior, there is a need for cross-cultural studies of aging and dying and for comparative studies of specialized institutions for the elderly which serve different racial and ethnic groups. There is also a need for comparative studies of the relations among social class, ethnic background, and life-styles of the elderly with regard to admissions trauma (Clark 1967).

The current emphasis in some American ethnic groups is on fostering ethnic identities; consequently recurring conflicts erupt at the interfaces of racial and ethnic groups. Sociocultural analyses of aging and social reactions to the elderly could therefore contribute to intergroup understanding as well as to the science of social gerontology by focusing more research and public reports on cross-cultural and comparative studies of racial and ethnic situations surrounding aging and dying.

Notes

1. There were 190 residents living in the black home in January 1973, the beginning of the eleven month period of observations that provided most of the data discussed in this chapter. By the middle of this period, a reduction of 8 percent or sixteen patients had occurred in the population of the home. The decrease was determined by resident mortalities without replacement and by an administrative decision to gradually reduce the overall number of residents served by the home. The 174 residents referred to earlier in this chapter constitute the number of persons in residence during most of the observational period and with whom most of the observed staff-resident interactions occurred.

2. These findings were culled from protocols of informant interviews done between October 1 and November 19, 1971.

3. At the time planned for data collection pertaining to this study there were staff–resident conflicts in the black home that influenced the administrators to deny permission for us to make direct observations of face-to-face interactions between nursing staff and elderly residents.

References

Aguilera, D. C. "Relationship Between Physical Contact and Verbal Inter-action Between Nurses and Patients." *Journal of Psychiatric Nursing* (January–February 1967).

Barker, R. G. *Ecological Psychology: Concepts and Methods for Studying the Environment of Human Behavior.* Stanford, Calif.: Stanford University Press, 1968.

————. *The Stream of Behavior.* New York: Appleton-Century-Crofts, 1963.

————, and L. S. Barker. "The Psychological Ecology of Old People in Midwest, Kansas, and Yoredale, Yorkshire." *Journal of Gerontology,* 16, 2 (April 1961a).

————, and ————. "Behavior Units for the Comparative Study of Cultures." In Bert Kaplan, ed. *Studying Personality Cross-culturally.* New York: Harper & Row, 1961b.

Bennet, Ruth. "Social Context—A Neglected Variable in Research on Aging." *Aging and Human Development,* 1, 2 (1970), 97–116.

Blauner, Robert. "Death and Social Structure." In Bernice L. Neugarten, ed. *Middle Age and Aging.* Chicago: University of Chicago Press, 1968.

Blenkner, M. "Environmental Change and the Aging Individual." *The Gerontologist,* 7 (1967), 101–105.

Cahn, Edgar S., ed. *Our Brother's Keeper: The Indian in White America.* Washington, D.C.: New Community Press, 1969.

Clark, Margaret. "The Anthropology of Aging: A New Area for Studies of Culture and Personality." *The Gerontologist,* 7, 1 (March 1967).

Du Bois, W. E. B. *The Souls of Black Folk.* Greenwich, Conn.: Fawcett Publications (1961), 1903.

Foucault, Michel. *Madness and Civilization: A History of Insanity in the Age of Reason.* New York: New American Library, 1965.

Glaser, Barney G., and Anselm L. Strauss. *Awareness of Dying.* Chicago: Aldine Press, 1965.

Goffman, E. *The Presentation of Self in Everyday Life.* New York: Doubleday-Anchor, 1959.

————. *Asylums.* New York: Anchor, 1961.

————. *Behavior in Public Places.* New York: Free Press, 1963.

————. "The Neglected Situation." *American Anthropologist,* 66, 6 (1964).

Jackson, J. J. "Social Gerontology and the Negro: A Review." *The Gerontologist,* 7, 3, Part I (September 1967), 168–178.

Kitano, H. H. L. *Race Relations.* Englewood Cliffs, N.J.: Prentice-Hall, 1974.

Lawton, M. P. "Prosthetic Architecture for Mentally Impaired Aged." Unpublished Summary and Progress Report, Philadelphia Geriatric Center, 1971.

————, and S. Yaffe. "Mortality, Morbidity and Voluntary Change of Residence by Older People." *J. American Geriatrics Society,* 18, 10 (1970), 813–831.

Lieberman, M. A. "Relationship of Mortality Rates to Entrance to a Home for the Aged." *Geriatrics,* 16 (1961), 515–519.

Maxwell, R. J., J. E. Bader, and W. H. Watson. "Territory and Self in a Geriatric Setting." *The Gerontologist,* 12, 4 (Winter 1972), 413–417.

Pastalan, Leon A., and Daniel H. Carson, eds. *Spatial Behavior of Older People.* Michigan: University of Michigan—Wayne State University, Institute of Gerontology, 1970.

Riley, M. W., M. E. Johnson, and A. Foner. *Aging and Society*, vol. 3: *A Sociology of Age Stratification*. New York: Russell Sage Foundation, 1971.

Rosebury, Theodor. *Life on Man*. New York: Viking Press, 1969.

Rosow, I. "Housing and Localities of the Aged." In *Patterns of Living and Housing of Middle-Aged and Older People: Proceedings of Research Conference*. Washington, D.C.: Department of Health, Education and Welfare, 1965, pp. 47–57.

Sigerist, Henry E. *Civilization and Disease*. Chicago: University of Chicago Press, 1943.

Sklare, Marshall. *America's Jews*. New York: Random House, 1971.

Stanton, Alfred H., and Morris S. Schwartz. *The Mental Hospital: A Study of Institutional Participation in Psychiatric Illness and Treatment*. New York: Basic Books, 1954.

Sudnow, David. *Passing On*. Englewood Cliffs, N.J.: Prentice-Hall, 1967.

Watson, Wilbur H. "Body Image and Staff-to-Resident Deportment in a Home for the Aged." *Aging and Human Development*, 1, 4 (October 1970), 345–359.

———. "Aging and Race." *Social Action*, 38, 3 (November 1971), 20–30.

———. "Body Idiom in Social Interaction: A Field Study of Geriatric Nursing." Unpublished Doctoral Dissertation, Department of Sociology, University of Pennsylvania, Philadelphia, 1972.

———. "Institutional Structures of Aging and Dying." In *Environmental Research and Aging*. Washington, D.C.: Gerontological Society, 1974.

———. "The Meanings of Touch: Geriatric Nursing." *Journal of Communication*, 37 (Summer 1975), 107–127.

Wax, Rosalie H., and Robert K. Thomas. "American Indians and White People." *Phylon*, 22, 4 (Winter 1961), 305–317.

Willems, Edwin P. "An Ecological Orientation in Psychology." *Merril Palmer Quarterly of Behavior and Development*, 11, 4 (1965), 317–343.

Worcester, Alfred. *The Care of the Aged, the Dying, and the Dead*. Springfield, Ill.: Charles C Thomas, 1961.

ELEMENTS IN THE 7
SOCIAL STRUCTURE
OF DYING

Segregation by competence in accord with some notion of adequacy seems a widespread phenomenon indeed. Performance criteria are embedded in all our activities, even in the smallest and most homogeneous group. We monitor each other's behavior, constantly discovering that proprieties are observed with a greater or lesser degree of consistency from person to person across time. Complex message systems in the form of words or actions help to maintain the conventional structures of encounters (Scheflen 1972: 104-121). Within limits, we cooperate with each other in order to prevent or gloss over small breaches of etiquette and to maintain the overall equilibrium of interaction. The tacit understanding is that we will help others to keep face and they will do the same for us (Goffman 1967: 29).

Slight gaffes may be overlooked or joked about. But in the event of an infraction of greater magnitude—one which is more difficult to ignore—the corrective processes may be more dramatic. Others may remark upon the event and offer the offender an opportunity to apologize or to account for the act in some other way (Goffman 1967: 19-23; Lyman and Scott 1968). To the extent that we are able to understand these implicit interactional rules and to cooperate with others in maintaining them, we are considered to have satisfied many of the obligations of social relationships. We become, in a sense, socialized human beings in good standing.

But what happens when the "hints and glances and tactful cues" are ignored or cannot be comprehended for what they are? What happens when our physical appearance or physiological functions begin to offend the character ideals of others?

> If the offence is great, the offended persons may withdraw from the encounter, or from future similar ones, allowing their withdrawal to be reinforced by the awe they may feel toward someone who breaks the ritual code. Or they may have the offender withdraw, so that no further communication can occur [Goffman 1967: 44].

There are of course situations from which the offended person is hard put to withdraw. It is difficult for the victim to withdraw from, say, a rapist or a skyjacker. It is difficult for the teacher to withdraw from the presence of an unruly child in the classroom, or for parents to withdraw from a retarded offspring, or offspring from depraved parents.

Where the threat to social order is great, one of the few practical solutions is to remove the offender from the presence of others. Human values that accent the importance of removing an offender help to explain the existence of psychiatric hospitals, nursing homes, homes for the aged, prisons, and other places of confinement. Administrators of these institutions may aim at the rehabilitation of inmates—but not necessarily.

Within institutions we may find that the exceptionally impaired are segregated from other inmates. Hospitals have intensive care units, homes for the elderly have regions for the severely disabled and near-dead, prisons have maximum security units.

One notes, inevitably, that often the supposedly clever are segregated from the supposedly stupid, the good from the bad, the hopeless from the improvable. It is observable in homes for the aged that old people are similarly segregated according to their degree of disability (Watson 1974). Segregation is usually such that old people who presumably need the least attention are so situated as to enable them to initiate interactions more readily with staff, visitors, and other residents, whereas the severely disabled are confined to geriatric chairs in remote corridors—which in effect puts them out of sight and symbolically out of mind (Watson 1974). The descriptions of the Jewish and the black homes for the elderly in the preceding chapters are consistent with the overall picture delineated here.

Since the hopelessly disabled elderly are segregated from those characterized by a higher level of functional competence, the first question is, why should this be so? The second question, which has more practical implications is, what happens to the residents who are segregated?

The Sick Role and Irreversible Illness

Chapter 5 dealt in detail with the concept of the sick role, with special reference to disabled elderly persons. We saw that the extremely disabled are ordinarily incapable of the psychomotor coordination involved in housekeeping, grooming, toileting, and ambulation. Most of them clearly require physical and behavioral changes if there is to be improvement. However, where there is extreme physical and mental disability, the elderly may be unable to show that they want to get well, much less actively seek the help of others in regaining their health (Watson 1976). In other words, even if they are capable of so complex a desire as wanting to get well, they may be unable to articulate it.

In the absence of an ability to articulate a need for professional help, it is easy for others to view the mentally disabled as people who not only don't want to get well but are too impaired to even recognize that they are ill. The elderly may also fail to express a wish to be well when they are unaware of the extent of their physical or mental deterioration. In either case, they risk being labeled and treated as hopeless, rather than improvable. They are consigned not to a sick role but to a doomed status, symbolized by their removal to a near-death group in a back region of their place of confinement.

Effects of Segregation on the Disabled Elderly

Segregation by competence has certain fairly obvious effects on old people, some positive and some negative. Segregation may have a positive effect on competent old people since it removes them from contact with the mentally impaired, whose behavior they are likely to find inappropriate and either puzzling or offensive, and whose presence is a more or less constant reminder of the state in which the competent *could* someday find themselves. Moreover, segregation maintains the competent in a comfortable but reasonably challenging social environment. For the highly impaired the effects of segregation may be more mixed. On the one hand, it may prevent the practice of whatever residual social skills remain and thus accelerate deterioration (Watson 1976). On the other hand, segregation functions to reduce the likelihood that the impaired resident will be placed in very competitive or otherwise anxiety-producing situations with more competent older persons ("How Well a Patient . . ." 1972; Maxwell, Bader, and Chaiffetz 1970).

We may follow our speculations about the role and the segregation of impaired old persons a bit farther. Let us try to imagine an analogous situation. A patient has entered a general hospital for observation. He has been in the ward for some time, chats with his neighbors, and is pretty much ignored by medical staff. Then one day he complains of chest pains. All at once there is a flurry of attending personnel, the patient is wheeled into a smaller room whose walls are lined with complicated electronic apparatus. He finds himself in an oxygen tent, strange suction cups attached to various parts of his body. Doctors hurry in every few minutes to listen to his heart, answering his earnest and increasingly urgent queries with transparent reassurances. Nurses stare at him through a window, obviously discussing him. The half-dozen other patients in his unit receive the same treatment except that, one by one, they disappear from sight behind a crowd of strangers dressed in green or white, the whole group then being enclosed by a transportable screen, and are finally wheeled out, covered by sheets. Once in a while, a nurse leans into the room and asks our patient: "Are you *still* feeling okay?" Our hypothetical patient doesn't need to know much about medical procedures in order to understand that the staff expect something serious to happen to him, and soon.

Similarly, how impaired do old people need to be before they are unable to realize that their transfer to an obscure back area, away from the busy ward routine and into the company of others who cannot speak or walk and cannot groom or toilet themselves, means that their condition is deteriorated and their status hopeless?

Intervention and Regressive Intervention in Professional Responses to the Severely Disabled

Defining illness as critical can have deleterious consequences, perhaps through the combined impact of two social processes: first, the entry into the patients' lives of an emergency team; second, the withdrawal of the patients from their familiar community, their kinsmen, friends, and neighbors, and the shared system of relationships from which they draw their identity.

THE EMERGENCY TEAM

The emergency team may be thought of as a system of specialists who by virtue of their superior knowledge, skills, or power exhibit a capacity for explaining and resolving critical situations in the lives of others. However, calling in the emergency team may have a paradoxical effect on sufferers since (1) its activities are directly aimed at promoting their welfare, but (2) its operations may be frightening to witness, (3) its presence may be worrisome, and (4) its very activation implies that the sufferers' future is considerably less certain than previously believed. There is some evidence to support this although it is controversial.

In a study designed to measure the effects of social work and nursing services for the elderly, participants were randomly assigned to one of three treatment conditions: (1) minimal services; (2) a moderately active health and welfare program; and (3) an intensive treatment program involving social work and public health nursing and the possibility of relocation in a more secure environment. A check of mortality rates during a follow-up study showed that, although the differences were not statistically significant, mortality rates were about four times as high in the intensive program as in the minimal one, and the middle group suffered a mortality rate twice that of the minimal treatment group (Blenkner 1967). For some old people, it may be that the more active and intrusive the emergency team, the more damaging its impact.

Emergency health care teams, intensive care wards, and the multifarious apparatus with which they are usually equipped clearly represent systems of social action aimed at intervention to reverse a patient's acute illness so that the patient can be returned to optimum health. However, as shown by the Blenkner study (1967), health team intervention may have the opposite effect.

In contrast to intervention systems, there are occasions when professional members of a health team may define a patient's illness as irreversible. Labeling an illness as irreversible means that the skills and technical equipment of the health professionals have had little or no effect on the illness. Following this redefinition of a patient's illness, regressive intervention may be manifest, initially by health professionals, then by health care assistants, and subsequently by family members.

REGRESSIVE INTERVENTION IN THE SOCIAL STRUCTURE OF DYING

Regressive intervention is the process of reducing the frequency of social commingling and gradually withdrawing the allocation of highly trained professionals and other resources from the organization of care for a person whose physical and/or mental processes are severely and irreversibly impaired.

The research reported in the foregoing chapters on comparative institutional and cross-cultural studies of social reactions to severely disabled elderly suggests that regressive intervention is a widespread social adaptation to severe and irreversible impairment. So far as it may warrant the status of a principle of probable social behavior, regressive intervention may be illustrated as shown in Figure 7-1.

In the case represented by Figure 7-1, regressive intervention begins following a prognosis or evaluation that a person's illness is technically irreversible. When the signs of illness cannot be altered despite the efforts of health professionals, there begins a gradual withdrawing of highly skilled personnel from the service of the patient. As we interpret Entralgo (1969) and others, social reactions that signify this process are consistent with ancient and modern ethics about the proper conduct of physicians when it is believed

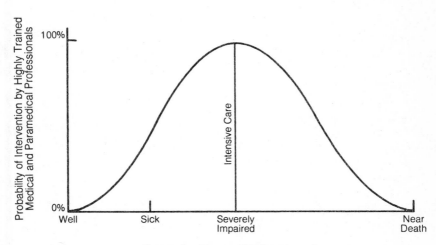

Prognosis of Irreversible Impairment or
Expectation of Increasingly Severe Impairment

Figure 7-1 THE REGRESSIVE INTERVENTION CURVE

that medical, surgical, and other techniques of intervention have failed to have any decisive effect toward arresting or reversing a course of illness. Through the denial by health professionals of the propriety of continuing to work as facilitators in a rehabilitative relationship, it is arguable that the patient's impairment and probable increasing disability become socially sanctioned, albeit by default. An inadvertent consequence of segregation through regressive intervention can be the acceleration of dying. Studies of sudden and unexplained deaths are suggestive of this conclusion.

CROSS-CULTURAL SUPPORT FOR THE IDEA OF SOCIALLY ACCELERATED DYING

Walter B. Cannon has hypothesized that the withdrawal of community support, along with the individual's own agreement that his condition is irreversible, may lead to shock and ultimately death (Cannon 1958; see also Hoeven 1956; Kraepelin 1904). Sudden and unexplained deaths—"voodoo deaths," to follow Cannon— contradict common-sense notions about dying.

In Australia, where the phenomenon seems not to be extraordinarily rare, the most potent method of lethally bewitching another person is with a pointing bone or stick, a sacred object which, after suitable ritual, is pointed or jerked in the direction of the target person by an accredited sorcerer. Frequently, this bone-pointing process has a profound emotional effect on the victim, who falls to the ground, slavering with fear, and is unable to move for some moments. (Presumably the victim needs first to be made aware that he has been bewitched.)

Bewitching another person can be problematic even among believers. For one thing, the assailant may not be sure exactly how potent the stick is, and there is always some danger that the evil influence may backfire, in the same way that the fifteenth-century arquebus and other ancient firearms were as likely to harm the user as the intended victim.

At the end of the last century, Spencer and Gillen (1899) observed a demonstration of the use of the pointing stick among the Aranda of Australia:

> After much persuasion an old man was induced to show how one particular type was used. Another native who was with them promptly retired to a safe distance, and the performer himself, after jerking the stick in the proper manner towards an imaginary victim, was himself rather

upset and said that some of the evil magic had gone into his own head [Elkin 1964: 293-294].

It may be worthwhile at this point to quote *in extenso* from the original report:

In addition to procuring death by giving an enemy a bone or stick it is a very common thing to charm a spear by singing over it. Any bone, stick, spear, etc. which has thus been "sung" is supposed to be endowed with what the natives call *Arungquiltha*, that is, magical poisonous properties, and any native who believes that he has been struck by, say, a charmed spear is almost sure to die whether the wound be slight or severe unless he be saved by the counter magic of a medicine man. . . . He simply lays down, refuses food and pines away. Not long ago a man from Barrow Creek received a slight wound in the groin. Though there was apparently nothing seriously the matter with him, still he persisted in saying that the spear had been charmed and that he must die, which accordingly he did in the course of a few days. Another man coming down to the Alice Springs from the Tennant Creek contracted a slight cold, but the local men told him that the members of a group about twelve miles away to the east had taken his heart out, and believing this to be so he simply laid himself down and wasted away. In a similar way a man at Charlotte Waters came to one of the authors with a slight spear wound in his back. He was assured that the wound was not serious, and it was dressed in the usual way. But he persisted in saying that the spear had been sung, and that though it could not be seen, in reality it had broken his back and he was going to die, which accordingly he did [Spencer and Gillen 1899: 537-538].

Cannon recounts some recent examples of the effects of these spells on Australian aborigines:

One day a Kanaka came to [Dr. P. S. Clarke's] hospital [in North Queensland] and told him he would die in a few days because a spell had been put upon him and nothing could be done to counteract it. The man had been known by Dr. Clarke for some time. He was given a very thorough examination, including an examination of the stool and the urine. All was found normal, but as he lay in bed he gradually grew weaker. Dr. Clarke called upon the foreman of the Kanakas to come to the hospital to give the man assurance, but on reaching the foot of the bed, the foreman leaned over, looked at the patient, and then turned to Dr. Clarke saying, "Yes, doctor, close up him he die" i.e., he is nearly dead. The next day, at 11 o'clock in the morning, he ceased to live. A post-mortem examination revealed nothing that could in any way account for the fatal outcome [Cannon 1958: 271].

Of course, the logical end of these beliefs is to treat the individual as if he were literally dead. For example:

> Some persons who are seriously ill and likely to die or who are so old that from the Melanesian point of view they are ready to die, are labeled by the word *mate*, which means "dead person." The label mate involves a degradation ceremony in which an elderly person is deprived of his rights and is literally "mortified." He is perceived "*as if* dead" and then buried [Murphy 1976: 1021].

A similar process has been reported among the Samoans:

> When an old man felt sick and infirm, and thought he was dying, he deliberately told his children and friends to get all ready and bury him. They yielded to his wishes, dug a round pit, wound a number of fine mats around his body, and lowered the poor old man into his grave in a sitting posture. His grave was filled up, and his dying groans drowned amid the weeping and wailing of the living [Turner 1884: 335–337].

Clearly there are dissimilarities between the situations of the Oceanians described in these passages and the severely disabled and segregated elderly in homes for the aged. In the first case, one finds a highly organized, quite explicit belief system, adhered to by the victim, the assailant, and the communities to which they belong. In the case of the elderly resident, the signaled messages are tacit, inadvertent, and probably not articulated by any of the persons involved. At the same time, the similarities are undeniable. Consider, for example, the manner in which the doomed Murngin of northwestern Arnhem Land, Australia, is treated by other members of the band to which he belongs:

> The community contracts; all people who stand in kinship relation with him withdraw their sustaining support. This means that all his fellows— everyone he knows—completely change their attitudes toward him and place him in a new category. He is now viewed as one who is more nearly in the realm of the sacred and taboo than in the world of the ordinary where the community finds itself. The organization of his social life has collapsed, and, no longer a member of the group, he is alone and isolated. The doomed man is in a situation from which the only escape is by death [Cannon 1958: 272].

His community draws away from him, leaving him alone, and suggests to him in countless ways that he is in fact doomed, his condition being irreversible. It takes little imagination to see the institutionalization of the impaired elderly, and their subsequent relegation to a ward for the severely disabled, as a similar process.

Something like the process described for the Murngin may account in part for the increased death rate following institutionalization of the aged, which, as noted in chapter 6, has been called transplantation shock or, more aptly, relocation effect (Camergo and Preston 1945; Lieberman 1961). The association between the relocation of old people and increased morbidity is rather well documented, although some old people seem to succumb to this sort of stress more readily than others—men, for example, more than women (Aldrich and Mendkoff 1963; Markus et al 1971), and those with chronic brain syndrome more than those who are psychotic (Blenkner 1967).

In the first year following relocation to a home, the death rates follow the pattern one has come to expect of postadmission rates (Blenkner 1967), that is, about half the deaths take place in the first three months and the other half are spaced about evenly over the other nine months. In other words, once an old person is removed from his community and relocated or institutionalized, he tends not to waste away gradually but to die quickly, the way bewitched Murngin do. We might mention that there are also some marginal cases of hex or autoprophetic death in Western society unrelated to the institutionalized elderly or those receiving intensive treatment (Wintrob 1972; Arieti and Meth 1959: 559).

The precise physiological mechanisms underlying death by suggestion cannot be determined, although it now seems likely that the hyperactivity of the sympathetico-adrenal system (Cannon 1958) or the parasympathetic nervous system (Richter 1957) is involved, perhaps both (Dynes 1969; Lester 1972). Sudden and unexplained deaths occur in economically developed countries as well as in the turn-of-the-century Australian outback, and it may be the case that there is a sociopsychogenic component in many deaths, sudden or otherwise, even when these are explainable in terms of an intervening illness. As Engel (1968) reports, a doomed individual has increased susceptibility to various diseases, and any pathogenic predispositions are more likely to appear and develop.

If unexplained deaths occur among young adults, as they apparently do, how much more readily must impaired old people yield, whose defenses against stress are already weakened and whose hold on life is already tenuous?

Summary and a Note on Ethics in Relation to Euthanasia

Unlike the ambivalent responses that intact old people evoke in us, the feelings aroused by the presence of severely disabled old people are often negative. This is a population indeed bereft of any capacity for rewarding others. When their behavioral and social deficits are so great that community services are called into play, impaired old people are likely to be treated at home, institutionalized, or segregated into wards inhabited by persons of an equal or greater degree of impairment. Once in a segregated unit for the irreversibly impaired, the disabled elderly are bombarded with stimuli suggesting, over and over, that they are doomed. But if they are doomed, and they and their families, guardians, and physicians know it, and if illness has made their existence physically painful or social rejection has made them emotionally depressed, then why not permit them to choose the option of ending their lives?[1] While this is clearly a matter of ethics, it warrants brief discussion here.

Ethics is the study of interpersonal conduct to which it is appropriate to apply the ascriptives *right* and *wrong*. In general, ethics encompasses any intentional act about which it is reasonable to assume (1) the initiator had anticipatory thought or advance knowledge about the consequences of the action, and (2) the conduct was believed to have the potential for affecting the well-being of another person (Reagan 1971: 7–10). An ethical issue is signified by differing or conflicting judgments made by two or more persons or groups, each point of view suggesting a divergent ascriptive about the character and the proper treatment of a person, such as a severely disabled elderly patient. Numerous ethical questions can be raised about social determinants of human aging and dying. Let us consider only one: euthanasia.

Dying as a way of gaining release from severe physical and mental impairment and feelings of social rejection is not uncommon. Suicide is sought often although all of its ramifications are not clearly understood. Euthanasia, however, is morally more problematical as it involves the participation of one or more persons who knowingly engage in ending the life of another who, often, seeks that conclusion.

Euthanasia is frequently referred to as *mercy killing*. Literally, it means "easy or painless death." There are two general types of euthanasia: one is voluntary; the other is involuntary, or compulsory. Voluntary euthanasia involves the will and consent of the patient along with the agreement of the family and/or doctor. When a person has a terminal illness, and suffering becomes intolerable the victim may choose to die before death occurs naturally. Involuntary or compulsory euthanasia does not involve any expressed preference for death. Instead, the decision may be made by family, friends, or others who believe that the patient would have welcomed death if the physical and/or mental capacity remained to ask for it.

Although the appropriateness of euthanasia has been debated for hundreds of years, the issues it raises seem far from settled. For example, the United States is a highly technological society with new medical and scientific achievements occurring at a rapid pace. Many conditions, such as kidney failure, that at one time proved fatal can now be alleviated, or at least death can be long delayed. The growing significance of issues about euthanasia and the nature of death and dying is partly a result of modern medical technology. For example, now that we have many means by which a person may be kept from dying, patients, parents, guardians, and physicians also have more responsibilities with respect to questions about whether a severely impaired person should be sustained in some life form or permitted to die (Fletcher 1960: 8–15).

We can prevent some deaths from cancerous growths and kidney failure; we can prolong their lives for days, weeks, months, even years with surgery, artificial respirators, dialysis units, and other mechanical devices. But should we? Thanks to medical and technological advances the average life span has increased steadily over the last several decades. But what are the characteristics of those saved lives whose maintenance has contributed to the increase in the average longevity for Americans? Some people have led personally pleasing and socially useful lives; others have been kept alive physically when no sign of mental coherence existed. Furthermore, maintaining a severely impaired person for an extended time under hospital and medical care poses serious financial problems. Hospital and medical costs that begin to diminish the life-styles of the well and impede their functioning may establish an apologia for euthanasia. A quote from Downing's study of euthanasia helps to make the point:

> There are many of us who would rather not outlive our usefulness, and become a burden to ourselves and to others. We must try to enlarge the

area of human freedom by winning for ourselves the right to die so far as is humanly possible in the circumstances of our choice, and for doctors the right to terminate life when they are certain that this is their patient's steadfast wish and that his condition is such that it should be carried out. If what matters is what the Greeks called "the good life," we should make sure that it can be lived by everyone to the very end [Downing 1970: 6-7].

Conclusions

Overall, this chapter has been focused on social segregation, regressive intervention, and a variety of related behaviors that are common social reactions to persons who seem severely and irreversibly impaired in physical and mental functioning. In addition to their spatial and social segregation from other patients, the severely impaired are often socially segregated from highly trained professional staff in health care settings. Coupled with the risk that the labeling as irreversible may have been premature is the likelihood that an administrative decision to deny a patient frequent opportunities for commingling with other patients and with health care workers may facilitate the patient's mental disorientation and physical deterioration. Social rejection of the severely impaired is tantamount to socially structured dying. Socially structured dying may be as deadly to the mind and emotion of a patient as irreversible biological deterioration is to the body.

However, not all severely impaired patients are given up with equal dispatch by health professionals, family members, and friends. Among the severely impaired in establishments designed for the delivery of health care in America, the rich and middle income patient, the white or Euroamerican patient, the youthful, and those who are believed to be mentally coherent are ordinarily treated well by professionally trained health care workers, with cautious considerations given to regressive intervention. By contrast, patients who are poor, black, or elderly and those who are believed to be mentally disoriented are treated by professional workers with a noticeable disregard for their integrity and are penalized by an earlier incidence of regressive intervention (*Double Jeopardy* 1964; Cahn 1969: 55-67).

While dying is one sure way of gaining release from severe and protracted illness and from social rejection, it is not always a socially approved option for the patient. Suicide, for example, is frowned upon and discouraged in the United States. Yet there are growing instances where patients, families, and doctors seek to provide the options for patient participation in securing release from a life of physical pain, rapidly diminishing mental abilities and/or outright social rejection. One of the great ethical issues of our times is suggested by the question: What are the circumstances under which a chronically and severely impaired person has a right to die, and who shall make the decision?

Notes

1. It might even be argued that this is sometimes consistent with the most important principle of the Hippocratic Creed—to do the patient no harm—since there are obviously circumstances under which a dignified natural death is preferable to continued living under artificial conditions.

References

Aldrich, C., and E. Mendkoff. "Relocation of the Aged and Disabled: A Mortality Study." *Journal of the American Geriatric Society*, 11 (1963), 185–194.

Arieti, S., and J. M. Meth. "Rare, Unclassifiable, Collective, and Exotic Psychotic Syndromes." In S. Arieti, ed. *American Handbook of Psychiatry*, vol. I, 1959.

Blenkner, M. "Environmental Change and the Aging Individual." *The Gerontologist*, 7, 2, Part I (1967), 101–105.

Cahn, Edgar S., ed. *Our Brother's Keeper: The Indian in White America.* New York: New Community Press, 1969.

Camergo, O., and G. H. Preston. "What Happens to Patients Who Are Hospitalized for the First Time When Over Sixty-Five Years of Age?" *American Journal of Psychiatry*, 102 (1945), 168–173.

Cannon, W. B. "Voodoo Death." In W. A. Lessa and E. Z. Vogt, eds. *Reader in Comparative Religion.* Evanston, Ill.: Row, Peterson (1942), 1958.

Double Jeopardy: The Older Negro in America Today. New York: National Urban League, 1964.

Downing, A. B., ed. *Euthanasia and the Right to Death.* New York: Humanities Press, 1970.

Dynes, J. B. "Sudden Death." *Diseases of the Nervous System*, 30 (1969), 24–28.

Elkin, A. P. *The Australian Aborigines.* New York: Doubleday-Anchor, 1964.

Engel, G. L. "A Life Setting Conducive to Illness." *Bulletin of the Menninger Clinic*, 32 (1968), 355–365.

Fletcher, Joseph. *Morals and Medicine.* Boston: Beacon Press, 1960.

Goffman, E. *Interaction Ritual.* New York: Doubleday-Anchor, 1967.

Hoeven, J. A. van der. "Psychiatrisch-neurologische Beobachtunger bei Papuas in New Guinea." *Archive Psychiatrie*, 194 (1956), 415.

"How Well a Patient Is Determines Where He Is." *Modern Nursing Homes*, 28, 3 (1972).

Kastenbaum, Robert. "Multiple Perspectives on a Geriatric 'Death Valley.'" *Community Mental Health Journal*, 3, 1 (1967), 21-29.

Kraepelin, E. "Vergleichende Psychiatrie," *Zentralblatt Nervenheilung und Psychiatrie*, 27 (1904), 433.

Lester, D. "Voodoo Death: Some New Thoughts on an Old Phenomenon." *American Anthropologist*, 74, 3 (1972), 386-390.

Lieberman, M. "The Relationship of Mortality Rates to Entrance to a Home for the Aged." *Geriatrics*, 16 (1961), 515-519.

Lyman, S. M., and M. B. Scott. "Accounts." *American Sociological Review*, 33, 1 (1968), 46-62.

Markus, E., M. Blenkne, M. Bloom, and T. Downs. "The Impact of Relocation upon Mortality Rates of Institutionalized Old Persons." *Journal of Gerontology*, 26, 4 (1971), 537-541.

Maxwell, R. J., J. E. Bader, and M. Chaiffetz. "Some Results of Intensive Recreational Therapy with the Mentally Impaired Aged." Paper Presented at the Gerontological Society Meetings, Toronto, Ontario, 1970.

Murphy, Jane M. "Psychiatric Labeling in Cross-Cultural Perspective." *Science*, 191, 4231 (1976), 1019-1028.

Reagan, Charles E. *Ethics for Scientific Researchers.* Springfield, Ill.: Charles C. Thomas, 1971.

Scheflen, A. E. *Body Language and the Social Order.* Englewood Cliffs, N.J.: Prentice-Hall, 1972.

Spencer, B., and F. J. Gillen. *The Native Tribes of Central Australia.* New York: Dover (1899), 1968.

Turner, G. *Samoa: A Hundred Years Ago and Long Before.* London: John Snow, 1884.

Watson, W. H. "Institutional Structures of Aging and Dying." In *Environmental Research and Aging.* Washington, D.C.: Gerontological Society, 1974.

———. "The Aging Sick and the Near Dead." *Omega—Journal of Death and Dying*, 7 (1976).

Wintrob, R. "Hex Deaths in the South." *Medical Opinion*, 1, 7 (1972).

EPILOGUE | 8

The studies presented in this volume range over a wide variety of theoretical, methodological, and substantive issues about human aging and dying. Although there are variations in focus from one chapter to the next, a common theme exists in studying the cultural and institutional influences on both individual and social reactions to aging and dying. The study of cultural and institutional variations with respect to human aging and dying constitute the core of sociocultural gerontology.

In the study of information control by the elderly, we saw that one of the most important variables determining their status and their treatment within their respective societies is the value assigned to that information by others. Social scientists' recognition of the function of the elderly as keepers of socially valuable information is not new (Simmons 1946; Cowgill and Holmes 1972). Nor is information-holding the only determinant of status and social approval for the elderly. For example, the greater the ability to acquire and maintain property and other symbols of wealth, the more socially acceptable will they be.[1] As long as the aging remain relatively free of severe physical and mental impairment they may generally function within the society with little loss of status. Serving as keepers for socially valuable information and as political and religious leaders in some communities are two ways of growing old without passing into a state of odiousness. But aging-related status passages are not always associated with judgments by others that their performances are socially acceptable.

Several factors may contribute to definitions of social aging, whether it is regarded as socially acceptable or unacceptable. Included among these factors is the social significance of change in physiological and mental functioning. In addition, social definitions and reactions to aging may be influenced by changes in family structure and by changes in institutional structure extraneous to family organization. For example, a change in the legal age for retirement could cut a family's elderly breadwinner off from a source of income, unless it is accompanied by a similar age change for old age benefits.

In societies characterized by youth-oriented and profit-oriented value systems, the elderly are especially subject to oppressive discriminatory treatment. The studies dealing with aging and race and with the institutional structures for aging and dying document some of these consequences of social oppression—particularly for the minority aged.

Whether aging and dying are studied (1) cross-culturally, (2) in specific societies, or (3) in specialized institutional settings, for a full understanding of these processes we must take into account decision making as used by the keepers of the elderly who judge and seek to regulate their social behavior. For example, we have shown that the old and sick do not necessarily acquire life-sustaining social and medical services. Depending on the extent and severity of illness the elderly fall from social grace; they may find themselves, or be found, socially and ecologically segregated, propelled into an accelerated process of dying socially—long before death occurs biologically.

Notes

1. Recent research by Silverman (1976) using 95 different societies demonstrates the cross-cultural validity of this conclusion.

References

Cowgill, D., and L. Holmes. *Aging and Modernization*. New York: Apple-ton–Century–Crofts, 1972.

Silverman, Philip. "Empirical Issues in the Anthropology of Aging." Paper presented at the American Anthropological Association Meetings, Washington, D.C., 1976.

Simmons, Leo W. "Attitudes Toward Aging and the Aged: Primitive Societies." *Journal of Gerontology*, 1, 1 (January 1946), 72–95.

INDEX